BOARD-WORK

BOARD-WORK

EDWIN CREER

ISBN: 978-93-5420-549-1

Published: 1887

LECTOR HOUSE LLP
E-MAIL: lectorpublishing@gmail.com

Yours truly,
Edwin Greer

BOARD-WORK;

OR
THE ART OF WIG-MAKING, ETC.
DESIGNED FOR THE USE OF HAIRDRESSERS
AND ESPECIALLY OF YOUNG MEN IN THE TRADE.
TO WHICH IS ADDED REMARKS UPON RAZORS,
RAZOR-SHARPENING, RAZOR STROPS, &
MISCELLANEOUS RECIPES,
SPECIALLY SELECTED.

BY

EDWIN CREER

EDITOR OF "THE HAIRDRESSERS' CHRONICLE,"
AUTHOR OF "A POPULAR TREATISE ON THE HUMAN HAIR,"
"LESSONS IN HAIRDRESSING," ETC.

WITH PORTRAIT AND NUMEROUS ILLUSTRATIONS.

1887

PREFACE.

The following work, which is the result of much anxious study and labour, is designed to meet a long-felt want. It is intended chiefly for the use of apprentices, improvers, and others in the trade whose knowledge of board-work is deficient. The Author trusts that the efforts he has thus made to disseminate sound and useful information will be appreciated by those for whom the book is intended. The greater portion of the matter has been already published in *The Hairdressers' Chronicle*, but for the purposes of this work it has been carefully collated, revised, and additions made, so that the subject might be presented to the trade in a complete form. Nothing of importance to learners has been omitted, and the Author has dwelt, with repeated emphasis, upon items which might be considered by some, as minor details; but every skilled workman knows how necessary it is for pupils to be well grounded in the rudiments of their art.

It may be taken for granted that he who habitually pays attention to small matters in connection with his business, will be the one most depended upon by his employer. But the advantage to be derived from such a course of action does not end here, for should he embark in trade, the careful and painstaking man is more likely to meet with a lasting success. "Anything worth doing, is worth doing well," cannot be too deeply impressed upon the mind, and those who studiously regard the maxim will take a pride in all they undertake. Undue haste in production must needs make careless workmen, and, perhaps, excessively keen competition lies at the bottom of all. The Author has reason to know that a fair percentage of the public does not object to giving a reasonable price for a good article, and it is worth while to cultivate such a class of customers. The tradesman, however, must first acquire ability in his special walk in life; no effort should be spared to secure the confidence of his patrons by upright dealing: thus it is that reputations are made and sustained. The public experiences no difficulty in procuring *cheap* articles; those which are good in quality and reasonable in price may not be so easily obtainable. All through this work, the Author has strenuously urged the reader to produce superior work as a tradesman, and to practise fair dealing as a man, and if these principles be acted upon, the student, for whose benefit this treatise is designed, cannot fail to profit by this endeavour to serve him.

When the present phases of business, and the keenness of competition are borne in mind, the importance of every person acquiring knowledge in his craft will at once be appreciated. In no sense more forcibly than this does the truth of the adage apply, that "Knowledge is power."

August, 1887.

CONTENTS

CHAPTER XIII.

CHAPTER XIV.

ILLUSTRATIONS.

The four pages of illustrations are supplied for the purpose of giving the learner some designs to work from, and, as fashions repeatedly change, the ability to make up sundry pieces of work is necessary and unquestionably useful.

A brief description of the illustrations will be found at the foot of each page.

BOARD-WORK, ETC.

CHAPTER I.

Introduction—A Scientific Description of Hair—Chinese and Japanese Hair—Chiffonier Hair—Waste Hair—Turned Hair—Combings—Best Quality Hair—The Hair Market in Brittany—Dr. Lindemann's Gregarine—The "Chignon Fungus"—Cuttings.

"Board-work," in the fullest extent of its signification, means all that which is done by clever hairdressers and wig-makers in the workshop and at the work-table. It comprises the cleaning and preparing of hair for the articles intended to be made; weaving; sewing and knotting; the making of fronts, bands, chignons, curls and twists of various descriptions; scalp-making; ladies' and gentlemen's wig-making; and numerous other matters of detail in connection with the subject. That a treatise on this subject is required there cannot be a doubt, for while haircutters and shavers continue to increase, the clever worker at the board, to a certain extent at least, is gradually disappearing. This may be considered a bold assertion, but it is true nevertheless. Let me give an illustration in support of this statement, and experienced men, doubtless, will coincide with my opinion.

It not unfrequently happens that when a youth has acquired a knowledge of men's haircutting and shaving, he thinks himself tolerably clever and able to get his living. If he be well proportioned and possess a kindly disposition, such a youth is sure to obtain the favourable consideration of customers, and come to believe, perhaps, that he is on the road to competency, if not to fortune. By the time he arrives at nineteen or twenty years of age he most likely desires a change, and seeks another place, and as he doubtless will get "a rise," some encouragement is given to his views by indiscreet acquaintances. Numerous advertisements constantly appear for "a good haircutter and shaver, with a knowledge of board-work," and the young man forthwith applies for the situation, and obtains it—the "knowledge of board-work" required being, not unfrequently, of a trivial and elementary character. And thus he goes on till opportunity offers for further advancement, or going into business, when he discovers the want of "technical instruction." Unfortunately, apprenticeship is thought to be "old-fashioned," and a lad now-a-days thinks he can acquire as much trade knowledge in four years as his master did in seven. But such an idea is, unmistakably, "a delusion and a snare," and thus it comes to pass that many men seek to acquire at thirty what they should have learnt ten or a dozen years before. The foregoing remarks would apply equally as well to other trades, and thoughtful men regard this aspect of affairs with some degree of anxiety and apprehension, hence the desire for "technical instruction," promoted as it is by some of the City Guilds.

I have reason to know that the book entitled "Lessons in Hairdressing" is highly appreciated by many, both employers and employed, and I trust that "Board-work," which I shall endeavour to make as complete as possible, will be equally as acceptable to the trade. The letterpress descriptions will be given in a comprehensive manner, and where the intricacies are somewhat complicated or obscure, well-drawn illustrations will accompany the text. To those who wish to take advantage of my labours, I will briefly say that no work, however well written and carefully put together, will impart ability without practice. Practice must be diligently pursued, and thoughtfully brought to bear on the instruction given, and a satisfactory result is sure to follow. As well might a person, after reading sundry works on music, and becoming acquainted with the significations contained therein, expect proficiency on a musical instrument, as for any one to think of making a wig after reading "how it's done." Proficiency in any art or trade can only be acquired by application and hard work. The information it will be my pleasure to afford, coupled with the industry and perseverance of the student, must produce one result, that being of an eminently satisfactory character.

Hair is the substance with which my readers have to deal, and the subject I have to write about. Hair—the theme of poets' song, and the ambition of all true artists to well depict on canvas. The crowning glory of woman is a fine head of hair, and baldness only becomes age. Were a person to ask, "What is hair?" probably nineteen people out of every twenty would consider him an ignoramus, but only let the querist press for a logical reply, and he, in turn, might regard others in a similar light. Those employed in manufacturing trades ought surely to know some particulars concerning the chief material used in the business in which they are engaged. Unless this knowledge be imparted to the apprentice or journeyman, technical instruction in any trade cannot be complete. Physicians and surgeons undergo a long and anxious training before they are qualified to deal with the numerous ills "that flesh is heir to." Dentists, aurists, ophthalmists, chemists, lawyers, and many others have to master the details of their respective occupations, before they are regarded as competent men.

It is somewhat surprising to witness the intelligence and knowledge brought to bear upon sundry manufactures, and a few visits to some of our workshops and hives of industry in London and the provinces, would prove a source of pleasure and instruction. I maintain that a scientific as well as practical knowledge of the materials used in any occupation, is essential to the welfare of the clever workman; therefore, before proceeding farther with the object I have in view, I consider it necessary to answer the question—*What is Hair?*

Hair is distributed over all parts of the body, with the exception of the palms of the hands, soles of the feet, and the lips. It grows abundantly upon the head and face, and sparingly upon the trunk and limbs, and according to its location, differences are observed in shape, size, colour, and structure. With reference to the structure, I may observe that a hair has three different modifications of tissue, viz., its centre, which constitutes the medulla, or pith, and is a loose cellulated tissue; that which encloses it forming a greater portion of a human hair called a fibrous tissue; and the outer sheath, cuticle or external surface, which is of a horny description. Hairs are somewhat cylindrical in shape, but not exactly round, and curly or waved hair is rather flat. Sometimes a hair is described as being hollow, but this is incorrect, for it not only has a cortical (or external) structure, but a medullary (or internal) substance. The first is similar to that which may be described as the bark of a tree, and the second to the pith of vegetable substances, the internal portions of feathers, or to the marrow in bones. But it is right to observe that when a hair is viewed under a microscope with a low power it appears dark at the sides and bright in the middle, and that appearance would convey the idea of hollowness. This impression prevailed for a length of time, and justified the humble barber in stating that "the 'air of the 'ed was a 'ollow tube." He simply reiterated a statement which other, and probably wiser, heads had given currency to. When the cortical structure of the human hair is examined it is found to be jagged like the teeth of a saw, and it is owing to this imbricated arrangement that hair feels rough to the touch when the hand is passed from point to root. The serrated appearance of hair is produced through the outer layer, or cuticle, being composed of flattened cells, or scales, which overlap each other like the scales of fishes, only they are not so regularly placed. The *medulla*, also, consists of a number of cells, which can be seen in hair that has been steeped for a time in soda or potash. These ceils are found to be angular or rounded, and if the immersion has not been too prolonged, will exhibit a nucleus, and one or more globules, or granules of fat. The medulla forms a dark line passing along the centre of the hair, and occupies about a fourth or a fifth of its thickness. The medullary line is absent in infants' hair, and in very fine light hair; it is present in strong hair, and is not difficult to trace in white or grey hair. Dr. Beigel observes, that "we may drive out the air contained in the central tube—as the medullary has likewise been called—and see it re-enter again under the microscope. Turpentine penetrates all parts of the hair which are filled by air, but its action is slow and requires some time. If we put, therefore, a hair into turpentine, and allow it to remain therein about twenty-four hours, and view it by the microscope, we find the central tube, which was black before being acted upon by turpentine, light,—perfectly transparent. But if we expose the hair again to a high temperature, the turpentine evaporates, and is replaced by air, consequently the central tube assumes its dark appearance again." It is said that "nature abhors a vacuum," and, it will perhaps be thought that the barber's description of a hair was not so very far removed from the truth after all.

This description of hair is extracted from a lecture which I delivered to the members of the British Hairdressers' Academy and their friends, at the Rooms, New Bond Street, a few years ago, and the importance of a correct knowledge of this branch of the subject will be apparent before my book is ended.

Every hairdresser knows that if his work is to be good, he must use only hair of the best quality in his business; Chinese hair, Japanese hair, "Chiffonier" hair, "Waste" hair, "Combings," "Root and Point" hair, or "Turned" hair, however cleverly it may be treated to produce fineness (being afterwards dyed perhaps to impart the desired shade or colour), can only bring forth one result, and that of an unsatisfactory character. Competition, and the desire for cheapness, fostered as it is by the encroachments of other trades, all tend to the manufacture of goods "to sell," regardless of any other consideration; and the introduction of inferior material and workmanship, might thus be accounted for.

The study of hair, and the condition it should be in when made up and offered for sale, is of such importance that I consider some further remarks on the subject necessary. "If a thing is worth doing at all it is worth doing well;" therefore I address myself to those who take an interest in the business and desire to improve it, more than I do to persons who vend almost anything "for a consideration." Allusion has been made to various qualities of human hair, and I refer to them again for the purpose of pointing out what should be avoided by respectable and reputable tradesmen. "Chinese" and "Japanese" hair is coarse, strong and abundant, and unsuited to the English people; but it can be treated so as to make it passable amongst persons of "economic" proclivities. One thing is certain, and that is, Chinese hair finds its way into the market, for in 1872 no less than 100,000 lbs. of human hair was received at Marseilles, the principal portion of which came from the Celestial Empire.

"Paris owns," says Mr. P. L. Simmonds, in his excellent book on "Waste Products and Undeveloped Substances," "among its street curiosities, a race as distinct from the elements of social life as the roving gipsies who have clung together and run over Europe for centuries. Consequently, its manners widely differ from those of the common run of mankind. These heteroclites are a species of night-birds of the human race; everything about them reminds you of dark shades and fantastic silhouettes; they sleep at daytime, and spring out of the earth when twilight sets; no one could say whence they come and whither they go.... They move about the deserted streets like a horde of phantoms; the lanterns they hold shine dimly and fluctuate to and fro in essentially supernatural zigzags. The chiffonier has a basket strapped to his shoulders; he creeps along the asphalte like a wolf in a sheepfold; whoever ignores his attributions would think him bent on grievous mischief; he holds an iron hook, and stops at every heap of rubbish. Parisians are still in the habit of accumulating their refuse before their doors. The iron hook goes to work busily in the cabbage-leaf, rag, and broken-glass hillocks, while the light of the lantern shows the basket-owner what is worth taking, and then the hook transfers the rubbish to the basket over the man's shoulder." Among the hundred and one things which these people find is "waste," or "chiffonier" hair: and regarding this I will make a quotation from another reliable source.

M. Alphonse Bouchard, writing on the subject in *The Hairdressers' Chronicle*, in the year 1873, and at a time when hair was scarce in consequence of the then prevailing fashion, says:—

"The hair that has fallen off is carefully collected by men who make this work their special business. They despise that which their brethren of the rag eagerly search for. Bones, rags of every description, fragments of crystal, broken glass, old iron, old newspapers, all these are neglected and despised by these specials. See them bent over a pile of rubbish, which often contains little else but cabbage refuse and a few broken corks. They bend over it and kneel over it as intently as if they were looking for the philosopher's stone, when suddenly we see them draw from the midst the little balls of hair which nearly every woman makes of the hair-combings....

"But let us follow M. Denizet, the author of a remarkable work on 'Waste Hair,' in these developments," continues M. Bouchard. "This writer tells us that the plaits or small chignons, and which are consequently cheap, weigh from 60 to 80 grammes, and that in every one of them there is contained hair from more than two hundred persons. The following is their origin and manufacture. In the issues of the toilet of these two hundred women of all ages and stations, the hair of the middle-class woman is first observed. These women are in the habit of rolling the combings over their fingers, then putting them into a small piece of paper, so that they do not fly away, and this hair is found in the sweepings of the house.... In the state in which the hair leaves the bag of the collector it seems good for nothing. People in general would not like to touch it, and yet of this refuse the cheap *postiches* are made which adorn the heads of persons who will not pay the price of hair cut off from the head."

In speaking of the several operations which this hair has to go through, my esteemed Parisian correspondent quotes M. Denizet almost verbatim.

"The waste, seemingly without value, is sold at six francs a kilogramme to wholesale dealers, who sell it again, just as it was purchased, at nine francs, to small manufacturers, who work it, and then it is sold to certain hair-merchants, who in their turn send it to small hairdressers, both at home and abroad. The work of the small manufacturer consists in five principal operations, which are:—1. *The Cleansing.*—The hair is rolled and twisted about in sawdust to free it from dirt, dust, and grease. It is then opened by hand. 2. *The Combing.*—The hair having been well disentangled, stretched, cleaned, and freed from grease, by means of black soap or certain chemical substances, is dried, and then combed in large cards with iron points, the same as are used for mattress-wool; this operation is done very carefully, to prevent the hair from being broken. 3. *Turning.*[1]—Starting upon the principle that the hair is a conical tube, which tapers off from the root to the point, a piece of hair of the thickness of a finger is rolled forwards and backwards between the hands. The piece elongates, the hair going in different directions, according as the root or point is situated. They are then easily separated, and put once again root to root and point to point, and this is the reason why it is called 'turned hair.' 4. *Classing.*—There are only three lengths made of this hair, that which is used for plaits, for chignons of all kinds, and for men's wigs. The refuse from these four operations is about half of the whole quantity in weight, and is good for nothing. 5. *Picking the Colour.*—This work requires the most patience, and is generally performed by women. It consists in dividing the hair according to colours. As there are seven principal colours and three lengths, each packet is divided into twenty-one portions. The shades are white, grey, black, brown, chestnut, blonde, and red. The lengths vary from twenty centimetres to seventy centimetres. Having passed through these different operations, the hair is ready for use in *postiches*."

---

[1] See page 19.

From about this time, then, "root and point" hair, "turned" hair, and so forth came into requisition, and English "combings" followed as a matter of course. Nowadays ladies save the "waste" hair which has been removed by the action of comb and brush, and when the mass has assumed somewhat large proportions it is taken to a hairdresser's to be made up, and emanates therefrom in the shape of a plait, twist, &c. To show that I am not alone in regarding the use of this inferior hair with aversion, I will quote the following from the *American Hairdresser and Perfumer*: —

"This fact alone, namely, the general and almost universal use of the filthy and unwieldy substitutes for first quality cut hair, known as 'Italian,' 'refined China,' 'unrefined China,' 'Georgia' (refined China under another name), and all the grades of 'second' and lower qualities, all this has done more towards disgusting our better class of people (those who have the means at command) with wearing false hair than any prevailing style or notion could have done."

There is much truth in this, and I commend the further consideration of the subject to the serious attention of all who desire to advance and benefit the trade.

Having given a description of hair, and spoken disapprovingly of the commoner sorts, I purpose considering the better qualities before dealing with more practical details. If the maker of an article wishes his work to be of a superior description he must necessarily confine himself to the use of good materials, and the fine quality of the hair used is of the greatest importance. I will observe that hair should always be cut from the head, for then it is in good condition and very different to the "dead" hair which is thrown off daily by most people, and is now well known under the common appellation of "combings." Hair of the best description is obtained from France and Italy, whence come sundry shades of black and brown. The first-named country, as well as Germany and Sweden, supplies the market with brown, light, flaxen, and red hair, while grey pieces are to be found in most parcels, consequently its source may be described as universal. There are regular "hair-harvests," and agents or collectors travel from place to place at certain times, for the purpose of obtaining the hair of peasant-girls in exchange for money, trinkets, or other articles of personal adornment. Mr. Francis Trollope, in his "Summer in Brittany," gives an amusing as well as interesting account of what he observed at a fair in Collenée, and its relation here will be appropriate. He says: — "What surprised me more than all, by the singularity and novelty of the thing, were the operations of the dealers in hair. In various parts of the motley crowd there were three or four purchasers of this commodity, who travel the country for the purpose of attending the fairs and buying the tresses of the peasant-girls. They have particularly fine hair, and frequently in the greatest abundance. I should have thought that female vanity would have effectually prevented such a traffic as this being carried to any extent; but there seemed to be no difficulty in finding beautiful heads of hair perfectly willing to sell. We saw several girls sheared, one after the other, like sheep, and as many more standing ready for the shears, with their caps in their hands, and their long hair combed out and hanging down to their waists. Some of the operators were men, and some women. By the side of the dealer was placed a large basket, into which every successive crop of hair, tied up into a wisp, was thrown. No doubt the reason of their indifference to their tresses on the part of the fair Bretonnes is to be found in the invariable mode which covers every head, from childhood upwards, with close caps, which entirely prevent any part of the hair from being seen, and, of course, as totally conceal the want of it. The money given for the hair is about twenty sous, or else a gaudy cotton handkerchief; they net immense profits by their trips through the country." This hair is, as I am informed, the finest and most silken black hair that can be procured.

Preparing hair requires careful manipulation, for unless it be properly cleaned and drawn off into the required lengths, the particular work in hand stands a chance of being spoiled. Only fancy making a silk or skin parting with hair that has been imperfectly cleaned; the result can easily be imagined; or a sensitive lady's surprise and disgust should she discover a "nit" upon her torsade or plait.

While mentioning this, I cannot help calling to mind the exaggerated and untruthful statements which were made some years ago in reference to Dr. Lindemann's alleged discovery of "gregarines" upon false hair, and their rapid procreation. The effect produced was most prejudicial to hairdressers, until, after a few weeks had elapsed, it came to be regarded as "one of those things which no fella could understand." Let me here observe that I have not seen a gregarine, neither have I been able to procure one from the source indicated by the learned Russian professor, nor could I ever meet with a scientific gentleman who had a specimen of the kind in his possession. Indeed, I might go a little farther, and say that I have been unable to discover any one who has even seen a gregarine, although the "Micrographic Dictionary" informs me that they are to be obtained from about eighty different sources. Such, then, is their insignificant character and appearance when viewed under a powerful glass. This scare was soon followed by the so-called "chignon fungus," which brought forth a most interesting disquisition upon the subject by Dr. Tilbury Fox, at one of the learned societies; but the fungoid growth that was found upon a particular piece of hair had nothing whatever to do with a chignon, as an examination of a portion of the same hair now in my possession would readily prove.

The good condition of hair is taken into consideration by professional hair merchants, for their very success in business depends on the unmistakably clean and glossy appearance of the article in which they deal. I would urge, therefore, all hairdressers who carry on a respectable trade, and are desirous of improving it, to purchase hair of first-rate quality only, and only to buy it of those who study to well prepare it for their use. They should avoid, if possible, having anything to do with the common rubbish which now and again finds its way into the market, and will thus be able to give a good article for a fair and remunerative price. It may be said, however, that all in the hairdressing profession are not able to go or send to some depôt in the vicinity for every little requirement; neither is it convenient for them to keep in stock hair of every shade or length. Besides, they may have a quantity of "cuttings" (not "combings," mark you!) which should be utilised and, after careful treatment, made up for sale. It is, then, to such tradesmen that I desire to speak, and hope my remarks will be found useful in the course of their business career.

CHAPTER II.

The Implements Used in Preparing Hair—The Preparation of Hair
Described—Washing the Hair—Drying the Hair—Drawing the
Hair—Nitting the Hair—Carding the Hair—Curling the Hair—
Boiling and Baking the Hair.

I will assume that the larger portion of my readers are well acquainted with the various implements and tools used in the trade, but as this book will, no doubt, be brought prominently under the notice of apprentices and improvers, a brief description of such things is not altogether unnecessary.

A "card" is made with a thick wooden base, into which a large number of steel prongs or spikes, about two or three inches deep, have been firmly set, and it is used for carding or smoothing hair. The possession of a pair of good drawing-brushes is also most important. They should be large and heavy, and well filled with the best bristles. These brushes are made of various sizes, but as they are so necessary and useful, I would recommend the purchase of a good article, and of fair proportions.[2] A "nitting machine" reminds one of a small-tooth comb, for its purpose is similar. It is made of brass, fitted with screws to be turned with the thumb and finger, and these hold together or open at will a closely-set number of steel teeth. This compact little instrument is intended to be fixed, when in use, to the front of the "card," so that the whole length of hair may be passed through it several times. A "jigger" is wanted when piping or curling hair. It is a piece of hard wood, about seven or eight inches long, three inches wide, and half-an-inch in thickness. There are to be three holes, in the form of a triangle, towards the upper end, through which ordinary screws are passed to fix it securely to the work-table or bench. About three inches of this piece of wood or "jigger" must be allowed to project, and through the projecting part two holes are to be made in a line with each other. A piece of strong string is to be passed through these two holes, tied in a knot, and extend to within a couple of inches of the floor. The "pipes," for curling hair, are about three-and-a-half inches in length, and the thickness of a lead pencil. Formerly they were made of earthenware clay, but common tobacco-pipe, pieces of cane, or, better still, willow, with the bark stripped off, answer every purpose. In addition to the foregoing, a dozen or more pieces of wood, about twelve or fifteen inches long and one inch square, will be required, together with vessels for boiling hair, tins or dishes for baking hair, plenty of string, a dressing comb or two, scissors, etc., and an old razor-blade, well-set in a handle, allowing two inches of

---

[2] For the convenience of those who desire the information, I may state that Messrs. R. Hovenden & Sons keep all the necessary implements in stock, and supply them to the trade.

the blade to appear, will all be useful. Soft soap, and some of the best Scotch soda, together with hot and cold water, must also be provided.

Let me suppose that the reader has a small stock of hair by him, which he is desirous of bringing into use. It may have been accumulating for some time, and is, probably, of divers lengths and colours. It should be collected together, and the first thing to do is to get the hair thoroughly clean, so as to prepare it for after manipulation. Separate the different qualities first, should there be any variation in that respect, and put all the coarse hair into one lot, and all the fine into another. In the event of a piece of hair being rather more bulky than the rest, divide it, so as to have each piece about the same size and not any thicker than can be washed and dried in an easy, as well as effectual manner. Tie every piece with string moderately tight and securely fastened, but loose enough for the tie to slide up and down a little when the hair is being washed, otherwise, some portion of the hair will be clean, and where tied, dirty. Before washing, it is better to give each piece a rough "carding," so as to prevent its matting together, and probably breaking the longer hair in its disentanglement.

The foregoing instructions having been attended to, provide two pails or basins of hot water — as hot as the hand can bear — and into each one put a tolerable quantity of soft-soap and soda — the best Scotch soda if it can be obtained. Place a few pieces of the hair into one vessel to soak, so that the dirt and grease upon it may be more easily removed. Take up one of the pieces, and holding it as a boy would a stick, between the thumb and fingers, commence rubbing it in washerwoman style, and, at the same time, working it gradually from one end to the other. Do not forget to slip the tie occasionally, and if this process be carefully performed, a great deal of the grease and dirt will have been removed. This imperfectly cleaned piece can then be passed into the second vessel. Proceed in the same way throughout, changing the water frequently, or as soon as it becomes foul and unfit for use. When all the hair has been washed twice in the manner described, clean the pails or basins, and fill them with fresh water — hot in one, and tepid in the other. This is for rinsing purposes, and the last water must not be soapy, for so long as that is the case other water must be procured. It is of the utmost importance to remove all grease, soap, or dirt from the hair, and the greatest particularity should be exercised in this preliminary operation.

The hair can be dried either in the sun, in a warm room, or before a fire. If in the sun, and, of course, in the open air, each piece should be fastened separately to a line, and left to blow about in the wind for a few hours, or, in other words, till it is quite dry. If the drying process be carried on in a warm room, let the hair hang near to the ceiling, and avoid making a dust: but should an oven, or drying before the fire, be more convenient, turn the hair frequently, and mind it does not get scorched or burnt. Both these operations having been duly attended to, see that the "card" and "drawing-brushes" are perfectly clean, for the next process is that of drawing the hair.

I must now imagine that the various shades have been selected and placed in different lots, such as natural blacks here, dark browns there, light browns, reds, greys, and other shades or particular colours in separate and convenient places.

Commence with the natural black hair. Take a piece and cut the string which binds it together, hold the hair by the roots firmly in the right hand, and make smooth by passing it gently through the "card" several times. It may be necessary to reverse it, but in that case hold it as near to the roots as possible, so as to avoid wasting the short and finer hair, which is to be found in every tress. Having done the carding, remove the top "drawing brush," and place the piece of hair upon the underneath one, the roots upon the brush, the points being free and inclined towards you. Repeat this with a second, third, or fourth piece of hair, until you have collected all of that particular shade together, or until the brush is conveniently full. Then place the other brush on the top, press down moderately tight, and put a rather heavy weight upon it. The brushes being before you, the length of them extending from left to right, the hair which is free being of varying lengths (say) from twenty inches up to the very short within the brushes, it is now ready to be "drawn." The workbench or table should be bound with hoop-iron, rising a quarter of an inch above the level, to form a "stop," so that the brushes, hair, and weights may not be pulled off. But if the table is not so made it will be necessary to provide a "stop" by means of nails or screws. I have previously alluded to a dozen or more pieces of wood (the length of the brushes), twelve or fifteen inches long, and one inch square, and now I will describe their use. Assuming the longest hair in the brushes to be twenty inches, four inches or more of which being securely held between them, it follows that fifteen or sixteen inches must be free. It is requisite to have the points of the hair projecting a little, and only a little, over the edge of the table. The "stop" being at or near the edge cannot act as a check, but by placing a sufficient number of these pieces of wood between the "stop" and the brushes, they, *i.e.,* the brushes, can be made secure at any distance required. Take the old razor blade already spoken of (which for convenience I will call a knife), and commence "drawing" the hair in small portions of, say, one or two hundred hairs. Continue this, holding the hair firmly in the left hand, while the knife is in the right, until a large quantity has been drawn off. As the length of the hair diminishes, so it will be necessary to remove one or more pieces of wood in order to keep the ends projecting, as I have said before, a little over the table's edge. Assuming that the brushes were tolerably well supplied with hair at the outset, the hand is likely to get filled three or four times, but each of these pieces of hair can be loosely tied for the present and put aside. It is to be noted that the fastening will in this case be at the points instead of at the roots, but that, I need hardly say, is simply for temporary convenience. The drawing-brushes being again clear, the same pieces are to have the tie cut and placed in regular order on the underneath brush—the longest hair being on the right, the shortest on the left, and the different lengths graduating between. Now put the other brush over all, with weights upon the top to hold the hair secure. Let a sufficient number of slips of wood fill up the vacancy between the "stop" and the brushes, while the ends of the longest hair project a little over the edge of the table. Remember that the *roots* of the hair are now before you, and commence. Keep the roots even and clubbed, but drawing until there is about a quarter of an ounce in the hand, when it should be neatly and securely tied. This is to be repeated until the whole of the hair placed in the brushes is finished. Of course, as the hair diminishes, one piece of wood after the other must be taken away, and tresses of certain definite lengths will be the result. These tresses can all be classified by putting the various lengths together, thus—seven and eight-inch hair (calling it eight), nine and ten-inch hair (calling it ten), eleven and twelve-inch hair (calling it twelve), and so on. The shortest and, in all probability, the finest hair in the brushes must also be drawn and firmly tied, but I purpose dealing with that, under the designation of "crop" hair, in due course. This process of drawing must be pursued, until the entire quantity is disposed of.

Having got the hair well washed, and in regular order, you must now make a careful examination to see whether there are any nits. This is important, for the most clever piece of work is spoiled in the estimation of people in general, should they discover anything of the kind upon even one of the hairs. To imagine that a mixed quantity of raw hair can be perfectly free from parasitic indications is a mistake which no respectable hairdresser would allow to occur. True, some hair goods are to be found in a condition the reverse of what they ought to be, but these are generally offered for sale, by not over-scrupulous tradesmen, and purchased by customers of strong economical tendencies. Be that as it may, it is requisite to examine the hair, and any unsatisfactory or suspected pieces should be picked out. Now, I will suppose that nits are observed upon half-a-dozen of these pieces, and with them I purpose dealing. Fix the "nitting machine" to the front of the "card" in a secure manner, and, to prevent accidents, it is most important this should be strictly attended to. Cut the tie: firmly grasp the tress of hair, and "card" it, taking good care that each time it is made to pass through the machine also. This is to be repeated until the nits are removed; the hair being reversed occasionally to "nit" the other end.

It is worthy of remark that the eggs or nits of the common louse are observable to the naked eye; they are of sugar-loaf form, and generally deposited upon the hair with the narrow end pointing to the scalp. Hence it follows that by "carding" the hair the reverse way the nits are much more easily removed by this useful little machine, which no hair-preparer should be without. The teeth of the machine can be rendered fine or coarse (as may be required) by means of thumb-screws attached, and this process being effectually performed, the hair is now ready for further manipulation.

Curled hair of ten, twelve, fourteen, and sixteen inches long, is most in request, but longer or shorter can be curled, if required. I have already described a piece of hard wood called a "jigger" projecting from the work-table, and some of the other requirements for "piping" or curling hair. These I will suppose have been provided, and sundry locks of hair selected. Take one of the pieces, say, for the sake of illustration, weighing about a quarter of an ounce, and see that it is well and securely tied. Moisten the right hand, and rub the roots together to cause the hair to "felt," and prevent the tie slipping. Place the tied part on the "jigger," hold it by means of the string which passes through, and press tight with the foot. By this means the hair is, as it were, held in a vice. Comb it out and divide in two portions. Take one of the pieces of willow, cane, or whatever may be employed for the purpose, technically called a "pipe," and a piece of rather stiff paper about 3 inches by 2. Put the "pipe" upon the hair, and the paper underneath, holding both in their places by means of the thumb and fingers and pressing gently the while. Draw the two downwards till you get to the points, and then commence to curl. By a movement of the hands, spread the hair a little, holding it firm and tight until it is all rolled up. Take about a yard of string and tie the hair and "pipe" together, by passing the string round one and then the other in such a way as to hold it firmly in its place without slipping, and fasten off securely. There is some art in doing this adroitly, which is difficult to explain in writing, but the reader should bear in mind that I am addressing those in the trade, and probably an opportunity will now and then offer for a practical illustration by some experienced hand. I have generally found it convenient to use all the straight hair in plaits, twists, etc., in the course of my business, and to purchase the curled hair ready prepared for use. This cannot always be done, especially by those who reside in distant parts, but a little practice will soon enable an intelligent workman to overcome any difficulty that presents itself.

After the hair is rolled or curled up on "pipes," it has to be boiled and baked, so as to "fix the curl." The hair should be boiled for an hour or more, and afterwards allowed a brief period to drain. While still warm it is to be put into trays or dishes and baked for several hours; there are suitable ovens constructed for the purpose now-a-days, but formerly the hair used to be embedded in dried sand and baked in a moderately cool baker's oven. The whole lot of hair is to be strung together like ropes of onions afterwards, and hung in a warm dry place for days or months till wanted. In unrolling (there being two curls to each tress) one curl should be turned to the right and the other to the left, and if this work be properly performed, the hair will present a bright, glossy appearance, with a natural-looking and durable ringlet curl.

CHAPTER III.

The Preparation of Hair (*continued*)—Crop Hair—A Remarkable Trial—Craping and Crimping the Hair—Inserted Stems—Boiling
and Baking *Crêped* Hair—Combings and Turned Hair alluded to
again.

The shortest and finest hair is employed for gentlemen's wigs, fringes, "Se-vigny" curls, and similar purposes. There is frequently a natural inclina-tion to curl in hair of this description, but when coarse and strong, it is best not to attempt to force it. To make the curl take one of the pieces of fine hair, and thoroughly wet it. Rub the roots with the palm of the hand as before, so as to cause it to "felt" together. Have ready a smooth brass tool, five or six inches long, and in shape resembling the end of a steel used for sharpening knives. With this (and the thumb) press the hair between, giving the hair, at the same time, two or three turns round the tool; draw away the instrument; hold the curl between the thumb and finger, and place it on an iron tray made for the purpose. Each curl is to be held in position by means of a small weight placed upon it, and there must be a "stop" in the centre of the tray to prevent the curl unwinding. The succeeding curl acts as a "stop" to its predecessor, and when the tray is full, it looks not unlike a dish of snails that has been prepared for some uncommon and remarkable feast. It is not possible to boil this hair, like that which is rolled upon "pipes" and securely fastened by means of pieces of string, therefore it must be steamed before it is baked. The steaming process can be done effectually in a small way with ordinary domestic utensils. Hair manufacturers would proceed somewhat differently, and necessarily so, because their work is extensive; but I am addressing myself to hair-dressers whose requirements are on a greatly reduced scale. Take a sufficiently large saucepan, and put therein one of those three-legged iron rings upon which meat is placed when sent to the oven. Every good housewife will know what I mean. On this stand put the tray containing the crop hair, and surround the whole with water, taking care, however, that none enters the tray. Put the lid on the saucepan; *boil* for at least a quarter of an hour, and by this simple arrangement the hair will be sufficiently well prepared for the baking process. Take the tray containing the hair carefully out, and after allowing the steam to blow off, a certain amount of dryness will follow, when it can be baked in a cool oven, or in front of a good fire—the oven of course being preferable. When quite cold the weights are to be removed, each curled lock of hair put into a box or drawer till wanted, and, above all, it must be kept in a warm, dry apartment.

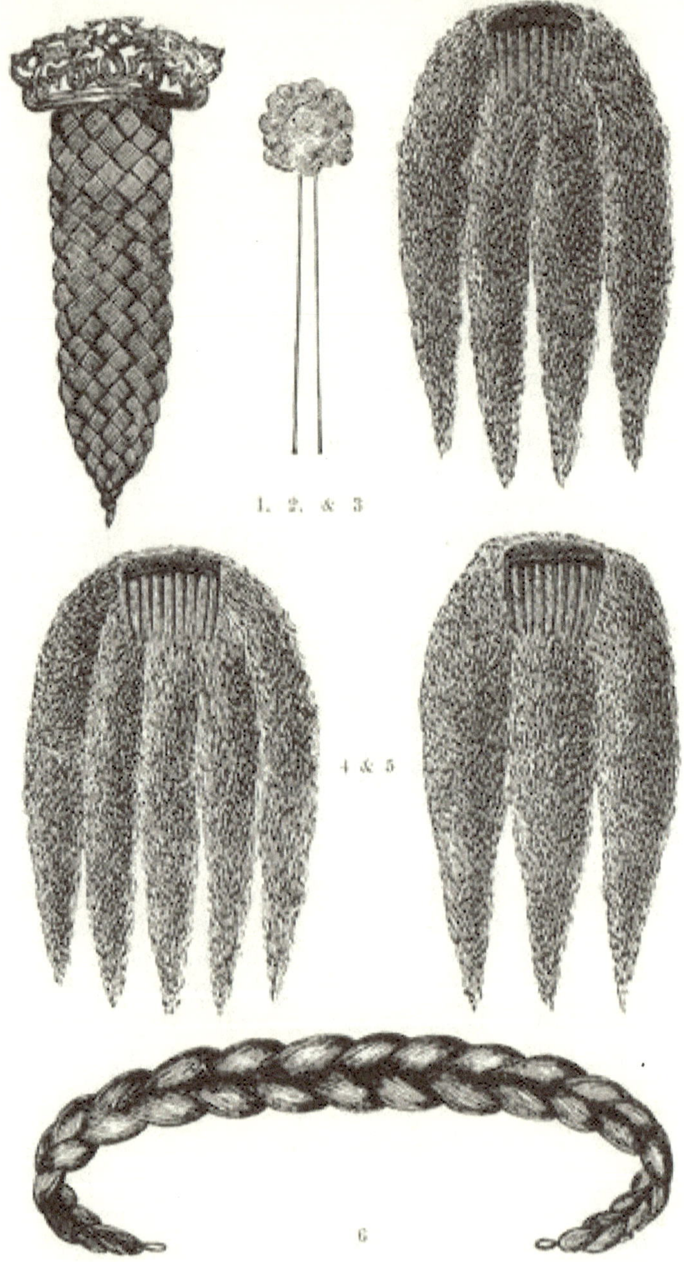

1. Seven Strand Plait, with Fancy Comb attached. 2. Pin Curl. These curls are generally made upon hair-pins, for which a small quantity of short frizzed, or curled hair, suffices. 3, 4, & 5. Human Hair Frizzetts, for plaited Chignons, Plicaturas, &c. 6. Long Plait, for a coiled Chignon when made upon the head.

When frizzets were used in the elaboration of a lady's coiffure, as was the practice a few years ago, several pieces of craped hair were all-important. The trade done in both large and small frizzets, pads, stems for *plicaturas*, twists, and plaits was something enormous, and quantities of a dyed material resembling hair were brought into requisition. And this was absolutely necessary, for the stock of human hair suitable for the purpose became exhausted. A brief allusion to the important case of Donisthorpe *v.* Jowett will not be out of place here, as it is largely connected with the subject. This action was tried in the Court of Exchequer, and lasted six or seven days, a full report of which appeared at the time.[3] It was an action brought for the infringement of a patent process which related to crimping hair, but more particularly applied to a dyed material largely used as a substitute. "I am afraid to mention to you," said Mr. Matthews, Q.C., in his opening address, "the figures that have been laid before me as to the extent of the trade. It is not pounds; it is not hundredweights; it is not tons nor hundreds of tons, but it is hundreds of thousands of tons in which this crimped hair is sold in the English market." But I need not stay to enter into the details of this remarkable suit; it is sufficient for my purpose to show the enormous business that was done in these goods at one time. I will turn, therefore, to the appliances which every hairdresser possesses, or can easily obtain, and deal with the crimping of human hair on a small scale. The method generally adopted for craping or crimping hair is as follows: Take the screws and pegs used in weaving (a description of which it is unnecessary to give, for the weaving-frame must be known to nearly every hairdresser or barber in the kingdom), and instead of silk, wind string around the peg made for the purpose. The string need not be thick, but it ought to be strong, and if a little stouter than ordinary shop-string, so much the better. When the frame is set up, two strings instead of three (the number usually employed in weaving), are required. Put the hair to be used in the brushes in the usual way, with sufficient weight thereon, and commence by drawing out a moderately thick piece of hair technically called "a weft." I will take it for granted that the reader knows what coarse weft is, in connection with weaving generally, and the "wefts" used in crimping hair are to be decidedly coarse. In this operation, then, the roots of the hair will be near the hand of the workman, while the length of the hair (whatever length it may be) lies smoothly between the two brushes. From the hair so placed draw out a weft, push the root-end close up to the knot (previously tied in the strings by way of a starting-point), and hold it firmly with the thumb and finger of the left hand. Commence then to intertwine the free ends of the hair, no matter how long it may be, in and out in a regular, firm, and secure manner. Let me suppose that you are going to crape some six or eight-inch hair, and that the root-end is being held between the strings as before described. I will assume that the free hair inclines towards the right hand, and is hanging down. Pass the root-end under the bottom string, draw it through between; turn it over the top one; draw the roots towards you again, and, by a kind of twist, change the position of the hair, holding the root-end (with the beginning of the *crêpé*) in the left hand, while the full length of the hair is free. This is to be intertwined in a regular manner with the string till the ends are reached. Push up close towards the commencement or root,

---

[3] *Vide The Hairdressers' Chronicle*, 15th July, 1876.

and use a "jockey" to keep it, as well as the end, in place. What is a "jockey"? It is generally a piece of wood, cardboard, or any other rather hard substance, used in weaving, and found necessary when the hair is coarse and strong. It is dexterously slipped between or upon the "silks," to keep the roots from springing up when each "weft" is placed in position. In this instance, I would suggest two pieces of firewood, about an inch and a half or two inches long, a quarter of an inch wide, and flat, tied securely together at the top, somewhat expanding at the bottom, and when made, to look like a miniature clothes-peg. With this little contrivance the end of the hair intertwined around the strings can be held in its place until the next "weft" is put in position, when it is to be removed, and proceed with the work as before described. This process should go on until all the hair is used, and there may be a yard, or any quantity of craped hair made ready for the next operation.

Hair of ten or twelve inches long is most suitable for making "inserted stems." Tie up two strings as before described, and knot them together at the commencement, which is the starting-point in intertwining the hair. The hair itself should be placed within the drawing brushes as before; pull out thick "wefts," and work them upon the strings as previously described, but with this difference, they are only to be crimped or *crêped* half way. Here is the mode of procedure—draw out a weft, and hold one half of the length in your left hand, while with the right you turn it over, and under, and between the strings in a methodical way, as I have previously mentioned. Push up each piece as it is worked, close and tight. Thus one half of the hair will be left hanging loose, while the other half when the operation is completed will be *crêpé* or crimped.

Assuming that the work is properly performed, the next important part is the boiling and baking of it. Having craped all that is to be done, cut down the strings, and tie the free ends securely together. Have ready a clean saucepan (it is best to keep one for the purpose) fill it with either hot or cold water, put the hair and string into it and *boil* for about a quarter of an hour. Then take it out, let the steam evaporate, and put it in a rather warm oven or before a good fire. It should be well baked, for the crimp is wanted to be durable; therefore, if kept in the oven for a day and night so much the better. It can then be allowed to remain on the strings till wanted.

1. A Coronet Plait. 2. "Catogan" Chignon; being a twist and four-strand plait, with ribbon bow. 3. The "Dolly Varden" headdress. 4. Marguerite Plaits; which can be made in any length of hair, and are easily formed into Coils, &c. 5. Semi-covered Stems, otherwise "inserted stems," for plaited Coils, Coronets, &c.

When the crimped hair is required for use — and I allude to the making of ordinary frizzets first — cut the strings at convenient places and pull them out. Have a "card" and "drawing brushes" handy, and as each piece is carded, spread it upon one of the brushes by means of a dressing comb, and when conveniently filled put the other brush on the top, with a sufficiently heavy weight to keep it in its place. I need hardly say that the points are to be within the brushes, while the root-ends must be left projecting out a little way, as that will be found necessary and convenient. With reference to the longer hair which has been prepared for making the inserted stems, a similar course is to be pursued. The plain or straight ends are to be within the brushes, while the roots as in the previous case, are to be left free, say, to the extent of half an inch. Having arrived at this point, the next step is to weave the hair, and the method of doing so will be described in due course. I will remark here, however, that in weaving hair for frizzettes inserted stems, &c., all the wefts must not be set one way, as in the case when hair is woven for wigs, fronts, and curls, but each weft must be set in a contrary direction, *i.e.*, one up and the other down. I shall be better able to describe this under the head of "Weaving," of which it will be necessary to give an illustration.[4]

There was a time, and not many years ago either, when such an announcement as "Combings made up, and the Hair turned" would have greatly astonished the trade and the public as well; but now that kind of work is done in nearly every hairdresser's establishment, be it large or small. I have before alluded to the use of "waste" hair or "combings" in the manufacture of *postiche*, as it is termed by Parisian coiffeurs, and "false hair" by the generality of people here, and expressed my aversion to its employment. Hair that is cast off by a law of nature, after illness, accouchements, and a variety of other causes, cannot by any possibility be made equal in appearance and quality to the hair which is cut off from healthy heads. Then there is the customary loss of hair about the autumn season, which may be regarded in a similar light to quadrupeds changing their coats, and to birds moulting. Hair of this description is generally withered and dry, through a want of sufficient nutrition, which is the primary cause of its decay. There is an old saying that "the value of a thing is just as much as it will bring"; and to ascertain the value of "combings" from a commercial point of view, let any one go to different shops and try to sell a paper-bagful. The experiment is not likely to be repeated. Like a true artist, I object to the use of inferior materials, for however good the workmanship may be, bad stuff will spoil the lot. I have another objection to make, for I consider that through the introduction of "combings" the sale of hair — good, clean, glossy hair — has fallen off, and the hairdresser's profits diminished in like proportion. Nevertheless, this inferior quality of hair is used, and how to treat it in the most satisfactory way, is what I have here to deal with.

In preparing this hair, which generally comes to hand in a matted and tangled state, the first thing to do is to "card" it, and this should be done with small pieces at a time. After which, these pieces must be laid together until the whole is finished. Tie it in bunches of a convenient thickness, and wash thoroughly as previously instructed. It is then to be dried and drawn off in the usual way. Mostly

---

[4] See illustration in Chapter V.

it is made up into the required article without "turning," but it is not suitable for curls unless it is "turned."

The process of turning hair is attended with some little trouble, and various tradesmen have different ways of doing it. Of course the hair can be worked better when it is turned, but, as cheapness is the order of the day, I suppose that where one piece of hair is "turned," nineteen other pieces do not undergo such careful manipulation. In order to deal with this part of the business properly, let me briefly recapitulate.

In describing the formation of hair, and speaking of the cuticle, or outer sheath, I have said that it is of a horny description; that hairs are somewhat cylindrical in shape (excepting curly or wavy hair, which is rather flat); that the cortical structure of human hair is jagged like the teeth of a saw, and that this serrated appearance is produced through the outer layer, or sheath, being composed of flattened cells or scales, which overlap each other like the scales of fishes. This can be *seen* by means of a good microscope, and *felt* in passing hair quickly from point to root through the fingers. By reversing the hair and drawing it through the fingers from root to point, the difference can more readily be detected in consequence of its smoothness. The knowledge of this structural arrangement is important as it bears largely upon the "turning" operation.

The combings are to be picked out and "carded," being at the same time held rather loosely in the hand. By so doing, the matted hair becomes disentangled, and is deposited in or upon the "card." It is then to be drawn out, piece by piece, and laid aside. When the whole has been "carded" in this way, it can be loosely tied in the middle, washed, and dried. I will now assume that the cleaned hair is before you, and that it is to be "turned." Place it in the brushes; draw off a convenient portion, taking care that the part held in the hand is clubbed, and proceed in either of the following ways:—Hold the piece of hair in the left hand, have a cup of warm water near, into which the fingers of the right hand are to be dipped as occasion requires. The hair is to be worked between the thumb and finger, and the peculiar formation of the hair gradually forces the roots upwards. These roots may be seen plainly with an ordinary magnifying glass; they can be easily discerned by those whose eyesight is good, and are to be discovered by the touch. They generally present a whitish appearance, and are bulbous in form. It should be borne in mind that I am speaking here of the roots in a business sense only, without any regard to the more minute scientific considerations. As the roots present themselves, the hairs to which they are attached are to be pulled out and "turned," *i.e.*, they are to be put at the bottom of the piece of hair in hand. As each portion is done, it is to be laid aside, until the whole is completed, the roots being at one end, the points at the other. To finish the turning process, the hair should then be drawn off and tied as previously described.

Several other ways of turning hair are adopted, but the principle is the same. Some use the "card" with the "nitting machine" attached. The teeth of the machine are allowed to be open or close, depending upon the coarse or fine quality of the hair, proceeding upon the principle that these "knobs," or roots, will offer a slight resistance and be intercepted in their course. Others, again, employ a row of needles, closely set together, with the same object in view, and producing a like result.

I observe that in a recent American work on the Hair, by C. Henri Leonard, M.D., the subject of hair "turning" has not escaped his notice. He says, speaking of the epidermal coat or cellular layer, that "the flat, quadrilateraloid cells forming it overlap each other, just as the tiles or shingles do each other on our houses," and that "this peculiarity of arrangement of the scales can be detected by the touch; thus, drawing the hair briskly through the fingers, from the tip to the root, it will then seem to be rough and uneven. Often, when quite firm pressure is used, a humming sound may be produced by this manœuvre. You can by this means always tell which is the root-end and which the tip end of the hair, as the overlapping layers lie *from* the roots. Now if you turn the hair, end for end, and draw it from the root to the tip, it will be felt to be smooth and even. Advantage has been taken of this fact by hair dealers and dressers, in arranging their stock. Where the hair has become disarranged, that is, a part with the roots one way and the remainder with the tips in the same direction, the whole is thrown upon a smooth, hard surface, and rolled briskly back and forth with the palm of the hand, or pulp of the fingers, when those with the roots in the same direction will begin to 'back out' from the mass, and then can be easily sorted out and arranged in a proper manner. Were this precaution not taken (to have the points all one way) the hair would never lie evenly and smoothly upon the head. This same 'rolling' process, in a minor degree, takes place at each twist of the head on the pillow, and hence explains why our ladies' hairs are less snarled and tangled than they would otherwise be after a night's repose."

CHAPTER IV.

Dyeing the Hair—Of Hair-dyes generally—Powder Dyes—Liquid
Dyes—Iron Dyes—Lead Dyes—Various opinions concerning the
use of Lead Dyes—Silver Dyes—Dyeing False and Faded Hair—
Bleaching and Blanching Hair.

Dyeing the hair *upon*, as well as *off*, the head, is a very important subject, and should be dealt with in as complete a manner as possible. A selected number of recipes will prove, doubtless, interesting as well as useful.

In the days of my apprenticeship—(it is not necessary to say how many years ago)—there were packets of "Pompeian Hair Dye" in the shop window of my master, which bore the name of the famous chemist ORFILA, and the recipe for making this dye was found, at least so the label stated, "among the ruins of Herculaneum." "What a wonderful discovery," I used to think; and "how I should like to know the secret of its manufacture." It was a powder dye, and had to be mixed with water, to the consistency of paste, before application, the hair being thoroughly washed and dried first. It was generally applied at night time, and the head had to be well covered with oiled-silk, a bladder, or some other non-porous substance, for hours, to confine the "mixture" to the hair. When the "bandages" were removed in the morning the head appeared as though it had been dipped in a flour-barrel; and, oh! what a task it was to get it clean. These powder-dyes are seldom used now; but, nevertheless, it is as well to give two or three recipes for making them. (1) Orfila's hair dye: Take three parts of litharge (oxide of lead) and two of quicklime, both in an impalpable powder, and mix them carefully. When used, a portion of the powder is mixed with hot water or milk, and applied to the hair, the part being afterwards enveloped in oil-skin or a cabbage-leaf for four or five hours. (2) Litharge two parts, slaked lime one part, chalk two parts, all finely powdered and accurately mixed. When required for use mix the powder with warm water, dip a brush into the mixture, and rub the hair well with it. After two hours let the hair be washed. (3) Litharge 4½ ozs., quicklime ¾ oz.; reduce to an impalpable powder, and pass it through a sieve. Keep it in a dry, close bottle. Wash the hair first with soap and water, then with tepid water; wipe it dry, and comb with a clean comb. Mix the dye in a saucer with hot water to the consistency of cream, and apply to the hair, beginning at the roots. Place over it four folds of brown paper, saturated with hot water, and drained till cool, and over this an oil-skin cap and a nightcap. Let it remain from four to eight hours, according to the shade required. When removed, oil the hair, but do not wet it for three or four days. There always was an objection to these powder-dyes through the time consumed in the operation, but the following act more quickly. (4) Take of lime (slaked by exposure to damp air) two parts; carbonate of lead (pure white lead) one part. Mix thoroughly, pass the mixture through a gauze sieve, and at once bottle it and keep the air from getting to it. Used as the preceding, but acts in one-third or one-fourth the time. The shade depends chiefly on the length of its application. (5) Chevallier: Take of fresh slaked lime 5 drachms; water, 1½ oz. Mix, strain through gauze, and pour the milky solution into a 4–oz. bottle. Next take of sugar of lead 5 drachms, water 3 ozs.; dissolve. Add to this solution dry slaked lime 1 drachm, and agitate them well together for a few minutes. Wash the resulting precipitate with a little distilled or soft water, drain, and add it to the "milk of lime" in the 4–oz. bottle. Lastly, shake the whole well together, and again before use, if it be not at once applied. It must be kept well corked, as the last, but acts more quickly.

I can imagine the reader expressing surprise after reading the foregoing; and to young men in the trade it would appear marvellous that people should submit to such an ordeal. That writers should condemn the use of "lead dyes" (if the last recipe given be the kind alluded to), I can very well understand; but liquid (lead) preparations I do not consider open to such disapprobation. One reason can be given why lead solutions are preferable, that is, they do not darken the skin; and, indeed, with liquid dyes in the hands of a careful manipulator, there is little occasion to touch the skin; but when such an accident occurs, it ought to be wiped off directly.

Liquid dyes are easily applied, more certain in their effect, and, undoubtedly, less unpleasant to those who have occasion to use them. Liquid dyes may be divided into two classes, namely, those which gradually darken the hair, and those which produce an instantaneous change. Before proceeding farther, it is advisable to note the chemical constituents of hair, because a successful result depends, to a certain extent, at least, upon this being taken into consideration and acted upon accordingly. It is known to scientific men that the chemical constituents of hair, according to the analysis of Vauquelin, are—animal matter in considerable proportion; a greenish black oil; a white concrete oil, in small quantity; phosphate of lime; carbonate of lime, a trace; oxide of manganese; iron, sulphur, and silex. Red hair contains a reddish oil, a large proportion of sulphur, and a small quantity of iron. White hair exhibits a white oil, with phosphate of magnesia. The white hair of old persons contains a maximum proportion of phosphate of lime. In preparing a dye for the hair, where the required element is absent it has to be supplied by art. For illustration, in red hair sulphur largely predominates, and as a consequence the hair readily darkens; in white hair—the white hair of aged persons—it is not to be found; hence the necessity of supplying a mordant to produce the desired effect.

To gradually darken the hair, then (assuming that sulphur is still developed in the course of its formation), a wash composed of a weak solution of the salts of iron, such as the sulphate, acetate, lactate, or protoiodide will be sufficient. A very small quantity of glycerine can be added at pleasure, but to the latter it is necessary. Here are two or three recipes:—(6) Sulphate of iron (green; crushed), 1 drachm; rectified spirit, 1 fluid oz.; oil of rosemary, 10 or 12 drops; pure soft water, ½ pint; agitate them together until solution and mixture are complete. Many persons substitute the strongest *old ale* for the "water" in the above. Another formula is, (7) take of rust of iron, 1 drachm; old ale (strongest), 1 pint; oil of rosemary, 12 or fifteen drops; put them into a bottle, very loosely corked, agitate daily for ten or twelve days, and then, after repose, decant the clear portion for use. The following is said to be a favourite among fashionable Parisians. (8) "Parisian." Take of sulphate of iron (green), 15 to 20 grains; distilled verdigris, 5 or 6 grains; white wine (good), ¼ pint; eau de Cologne (to scent), q.s.; mix. It should be mentioned that all these washes will "iron-mould" linen if they are brought in contact. Should the foregoing not answer satisfactorily, the cause will probably arise through the absence of the normal sulphur of the hair, and in that case, water containing a little sulphuret of potassium, or hydrosulphuret of ammonia should be used once or twice a week.

Much has been said concerning lead dyes, and the injurious effects produced upon individuals who have used them for any length of time. Dr. Benjamin Godfrey, a gentleman with whom I had the honour of being acquainted, devoted considerable attention to this question, and in his treatise on "Diseases of Hair," published in 1872, says: "The common hair cosmetics of the present day contain lead. The following is a rough analysis of the more noted:—

"Mrs. S. A. Allen's World's Hair Restorer, acetate of lead, sulphur and glycerine.

"Rossetter's Hair Restorer, ditto.

"Simeon's American Hair Restorer, ditto.

"Hall's Vegetable Sicilian Hair Renewer, ditto.

"Aqua Amarella, ditto.

"Helmsley's Celebrated Hair Restorer, ditto.

"Melmoth's Oxford Hair Restorer, ditto.

"Alex. Ross's Great Hair Restorer, oxide of lead, carbonate of lead, and potash.

"The quantity of lead in any of these could not possibly do harm. The strongest contained but ninety grains to the half-pint of water, the weakest but three grains to a like bulk. Water was the chief ingredient of them all. Sulphur, sometimes in the form of milk of sulphur, was used; in another, the common flower of sulphur; sometimes acetate of lead, at other times oxide of that metal. In all the chemical change is the same, namely, the solution of the metal entering into the filament by absorption, there unites with sulphur, forming a sulphuret of the material used. Hair is porous; sulphur exists in hair of all colours, but is in excess in red and blonde hair. This is why these hues become blackened by the chemicals used more perfectly than any other shades.

"Now, the question has been asked oftentimes, whether the use of lead solutions as hair-dyes be prejudicial to health or no?

"As this is a question of much importance, we will look carefully into the matter.

"The absorbent power of the skin is not great without we remove its outer covering. If we desire to get remedies absorbed into the system, we first blister the surface, remove the outer covering, then sprinkle our drugs upon the derma, and the material then goes into the body. In the endermic method of giving medicines, we must perforate the skin to produce any effect. The cuticle is the protecting agent—one of Dame Nature's waterproof coverings to keep out external poisons."

And again—"Now, the skin of the head is additionally protected by an oily solution—the sebaceous secretion—which forbids entirely the absorption of any watery hair-dye. So, protected with nature's waterproof cape and oiled epidermis, it is impossible for an aqueous solution to enter the body and destroy life. I have carefully analysed the cases recorded in which lead cosmetics are said to have caused death. Almost all the cases occurred in France, and lead, in an ointment, had been used. Now, an unguent could easily be absorbed by an oily skin; therefore these accidents are at least probable. The watery solutions of lead for the last ten years have been used largely by thousands and tens of thousands of beings in our land, yet not one single case has been recorded of poisoning from their use.... I have seen patients who have used lead dyes for twenty years, but not a single sign of lead poisoning has been revealed.... In the strongest hair-dye that I have examined there has been but one quarter of an ounce in a half-pint bottle of water, which would last the patient at least a month. Putting all these things together, one can state *that the hair-dyes, as used in England at the present day, cannot prove injurious to the users.*"

Another writer, Dr. Southwood Smith, in his "Philosophy of Health," stated that, "Over the external surface of the body, or the skin, there is spread a thin layer of solid, inorganic, insensible matter, like a varnish of india-rubber. The obvious effect of such a barrier placed between the external surface of the body and external objects is to moderate the entrance of substances from without. Hence the impunity with which the most deadly poisons may remain in contact with the skin, with which prussic acid, arsenic, corrosive sublimate, may be touched and handled."

And Sir Erasmus Wilson, F.R.S., writes: "The epidermis acts as an impediment to absorption, and as such is an important safeguard against the admission of injurious and poisonous substances into the blood. Thus we find that it is only after long soaking, or by continued friction, that we are enabled to overcome this natural defence, and then only to a very partial extent."

Of lead dyes the following recipes may be found acceptable—(9) Brown hair dye: Acetate of lead, 2 drachms; hyposulphite of soda, 1 drachm; rose-water, 14 ozs.; glycerine, 2 ozs.; dissolve the acetate of lead and hyposulphite in separate portions of the rose-water; filter separately, mix the solutions, and add the glycerine. The two following are from Dr. C. H. Leonard's work on "The Hair": (10) Sugar of lead, 40 grains; distilled water, 2 ozs.; apply this to the hair thoroughly, and when about dry apply a solution of the sulphide of ammonium, about one-fourth the strength of the British Pharmacopœia solution. The objection to this is its unpleasant odour. It gives, though, an excellent brown or black colour to the hair, according to the strength of the solutions employed, and does not stain the scalp.

(11) Brown hair-dye: Acetate of lead, ½ drachm; flowers of sulphur, 1 drachm; water, 4 ozs.; shake well and apply night and morning for a week or so, then decrease the frequency of the application, gradually, to once a week, or once in two weeks. This is a slow dye, yet one that answers fairly when there is not much greyness in the hair. It also is a very mild preparation. The deposit left upon the skin can be easily brushed off when it becomes dry. Like all of the lead dyes, it acts best upon hair of a reddish tinge, though grey hair is turned to a brownish colour by it. Its effect upon light hair is to give more of a dark brown tint to it.

I now offer some remarks on silver dyes, for probably they are more in use than any of the other kinds. One reason is, they are quicker in their action, and, with careful manipulation, more decided in effect. Before application, however (indeed, before any dye can be effective), it is important to thoroughly wash the hair with soda or soap and water, which must be well rinsed out with plenty of tepid or cold water, and the hair dried. It is then ready for the dye. It should be borne in mind that silver dyes will stain linen, the skin, and finger nails, and almost any thing the dye is brought in contact with. Under these circumstances, then, carefulness must be observed. Sunlight, and the open air will produce a permanent change in a few minutes; with diffused daylight it takes much longer, perhaps two or three hours. But science has stepped in, and, with the employment of a good mordant, the desired alteration of colour is effected almost instantaneously. Should the skin, however, be wetted with any of the dye, wipe it off directly, for if left untouched, a dark mark will be the result. A cloth damped with a solution of hydrosulphuret of ammonia, or sulphuret of potassium, and rubbed on the spots, will remove recent marks. So will a solution of iodide or cyanide of potassium, but these, on account of their poisonous qualities, are best avoided. Proper caution in using the dye, a pair of old gloves to cover the hands, and some little practical experience will prevent any unpleasant results. (12) One solution, crystallised nitrate of silver, 1 drachm; gum arabic, 1 drachm; distilled water, 2 ozs.; mix. (13) Another: one solution, nitrate of silver, 192 grains; distilled water, 8 ozs. Dissolve and add gradually sufficient of the strongest solution of ammonia to precipitate the silver. Then, afterwards, just as much as is necessary to redissolve the precipitate.

The following dyes require two solutions, and produce a rapid change: (14) No. 1. Hydrosulphate of ammonia, 1 oz.; solution of potash, 3 drachms; distilled water, 1 oz.; mix. Apply this with a tooth-brush, and in about a quarter of an hour use.—No. 2. Nitrate of silver, 1 drachm; distilled water, 2 ozs. In all cases when two liquids are employed, the vessels into which they are poured, the brushes used for applying them, combs, etc., must be kept separate, otherwise the action of the dye upon the hair will be destroyed. Generally, the mordant is used first and the dye afterwards, but this order is reversed in the following "Instantaneous Hair Dye," the recipe for making which is taken from the work by Mr. A. J. Cooley. (15) The white liquid, or "dye," is a solution of *nitrate of silver* (1 to 8, 12 to 16). This is applied first. It is followed by the "mordant" (diluted). The latter is usually a mixture of *hydrosulphuret of ammonia* and *distilled water*, in nearly equal proportions. The colour of the hair, unaltered by the silver solution, instantly turns "brown" or "black," according to the strength of the dye, when moistened with the hydrosulphuret. Then there are "vegetable dyes," "vegeto-mineral dyes," "animal dyes," "pommade dyes," and washes for producing red, auburn, golden, golden brown, and other shades of colour in the hair, but to go fully into this subject at the present moment, would be a little beside the object I have in view.

I might dismiss the subject of dyeing "false hair," as it is called, with a few brief remarks, seeing that hairdressers rarely think it worth their while to perform the experiment; but, as it sometimes happens, new hair has to be added to that which is old and faded, to meet the requirements of economical customers, then "how to restore it" becomes a question. Of course, if the hair be impoverished, and assumes a "foxy" hue, it cannot be restored; but—what answers the purpose just as well—it can be dyed. There is only one other reason to be adduced, so far as I can tell, for dyeing "false hair," and that is, when a tradesman has a quantity of red hair by him which is unsaleable, and, consequently, thinks proper to make it a more common colour. Whether red-haired people have generally "good crops," or whether they darken their hair by the use of suitable preparations, I will not pretend to say; but certainly red hair is not very often in request. White, grey, auburn, flaxen, and several choice pale colours are too valuable to be interfered with, and ordinary colours are sufficiently plentiful without resorting to the use of dye.

To dye "false hair," then, one of the lead and sulphur dyes mentioned in the preceding pages will answer every purpose, and its action may, in some instances, be promoted by boiling. Or any of the methods used in dyeing wool may be employed with good effect, for, in this connection, there is not much dissimilarity in hair and wool, and what will dye one will dye the other. In dyeing blacks, and dark colours, logwood forms one of the principal ingredients, and in conjunction with gallnuts it imparts a lustrous appearance. It should be used either hot or boiling, according to the depth of colour required. The accompanying formula is very effective. (16) Logwood, ¼ lb.; copperas (sulphate of iron), 1 oz.; nut galls, 1 oz.; and about 2 quarts of water. Boil for an hour, or longer according to the shade required. It is necessary to observe that the hair should be taken out of the dye-bath several times, and freely exposed to the air. This is called "airing," and is done to allow the oxygen of the atmosphere to act upon the ingredients of the dye, and especially on the iron; as without this action of the air a good colour cannot be produced.

To possess a head of hair of the "golden" *blonde*, flaxen, or auburn hue, has been the desire of many ladies from time immemorial, and various expedients have been resorted to to produce the desired effect. At the present moment I do not intend to dilate upon this subject, but of all substances used for the purpose of bleaching or blanching hair, whether it be upon or off the head, nothing surpasses peroxide of hydrogen, respecting which Mr. Alfred H. Mason says:—"The best known application for peroxide of hydrogen is probably in its employment as an auricome for bleaching dark coloured hair, producing the yellow tint: for this purpose a 10-volume solution is used, the hair is saturated with it, and then exposed for two or three days, when the oxygen is liberated and the hair partly decolourised; if wanted in a shorter time, after immersion the hair is dried in a water-bath for a few hours, but the ultimate result is not so satisfactory. A London hairdresser produces white hair, and it is conjectured that he employs a 20–volume solution, with the addition of strong solution of ammonia, and so completely decolourises and bleaches the hair, at the same time rendering it practically destroyed excepting so long as it holds together."

I think enough has been said upon dyeing, to enable the intelligent reader to overcome many of the difficulties that are sure to arise in the course of his business pursuits. The operation, whether it be performed upon the growing hair, or upon that which is faded and dead, must be carried out with carefulness and patience to ensure a satisfactory result. Men in all branches of science, have to perform one experiment after another before they can achieve success, and hairdressers, if they wish to be clever in their profession, must be content to do the same.

CHAPTER V.

The First Lesson in Wig-making, Weaving the Hair—"Once In," Close
or Ringlet Weft—"Twice In," or Front Weft—"Thrice In," Crop, or
Wig Weft—"Fly" Weft, for Top rows—Making Ringlet Bunches—
Tufts—Curls on Combs—Alexandra Curls.

I now approach the second and, perhaps, most important part of my work,
viz., the art of Wig-making, and under that heading I intend dealing with
the manufacture of Ringlets; "Tails," Twists, or Switches; Plaits; Bandeaux; Fronts;
Chignons; Scalpettes; Fillets; Scalps; Wigs; and, in short, everything which apper-
tains to this branch of the business. Weaving is one of the first lessons which a
boy has to learn in a hairdresser's shop where "a knowledge of board-work is
required." No matter whether he is employed in a first-class establishment where
superior work has to be done, or in a shop of less pretension, good weaving should
be aimed at, and demands primary consideration. In some of the principal houses,
professional weavers are engaged, who take the hair home with them, and bring
it back when completed, receiving so much per yard for their labour, the price
being regulated by the kind of weft made. This practice is generally pursued, for
assistants have not much time or inclination to weave, their services being more
valuable, so this operation is confided to other and less skilful hands; but whoever
does it, or wherever it is done, excellence should always be aimed at.

Every hairdresser is more or less acquainted with the weaving-frame, therefore I need not give particular instructions in reference thereto. Besides, the accompanying illustration indicates nearly all that I would say about it.

Fig. 1.

From the above it will be seen that the hair to be woven is placed in the brushes which lie upon the table; the roots allowed to project a little, and convenient to the workman's hand. The three "strings" as they are sometimes called, are in reality silk, one skein of weaving-silk being wound round each groove of the weaving-peg. The silk can be had either fine, medium, or coarse, according to the taste or requirement of the user. A tack is generally driven into the other peg (to which the "silks," by means of a loop, are attached) and around it the weft is wound as it increases in quantity, or occasion may demand. When the "frame" is in position, all the silks ought to be of an equal degree of tension—neither too tight nor yet too slack; and a "jockey" should be provided in the event of its being wanted. Do not bear heavily upon the silks in a clumsy manner; avoid weaving too much in one place, and as the weft lengthens, work higher up, towards the weaving peg. By observing these rules you may escape the annoyance of the silks breaking—a vexatious mishap, which sometimes necessitates undoing that which is done, and re-weaving it. Should a silk break, however, you must tie it close to the last weft, but there is a particular way of fastening which can easily be shown but is awkward to describe.

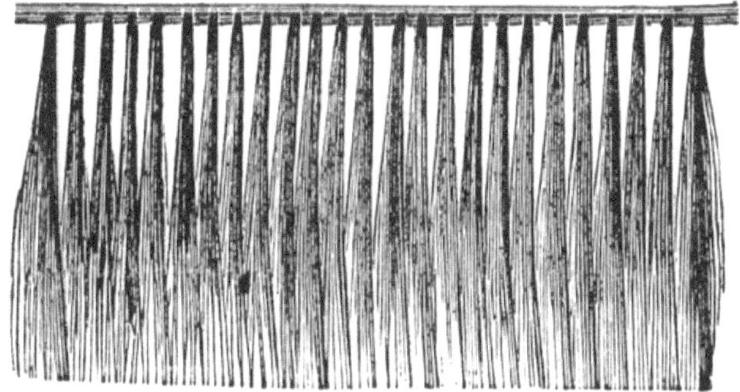

Fig. 2.

"Once In" weft, which has several designations, and is also indicated by the letter N, is chiefly used when a moderate quantity of hair is required to be put together in a small compass. It is employed for "top-rows," "bunches" or "tufts," "twists" or "tails," plaits, chignons, etc. To enable the reader more easily to comprehend the *modus operandi*, I will for the sake of convenience number the silks 1, 2, 3, beginning at the bottom. On the next page an illustration of the weft is given, to do which proceed as follows. Draw out a weft and hold it firmly between the thumb and finger of the left hand. Also, gather the silks together as indicated in Fig. 1, and with the index finger of the right hand push the roots between 1 and 2, and draw them towards you between 2 and 3. Turn the root over the top silk; draw it between 3 and 2; pass it under 1 and 2, drawing it through 3 and 2 again. Finally, turn the roots over the top and draw them between the two lower silks. Then hold the longest portion of the hair with the thumb and finger of the left hand, firmly hold the roots in a similar manner with the right, and draw them up as close, *i.e.*, as short as possible to the silks, at the same time sliding the weft down to its destination, as shown in the first engraving. Push up close with the thumb and finger of the right hand, and, should the hair be stubborn, it will be necessary to use the "jockey," of which I spoke before. This procedure appears somewhat difficult to the uninitiated, no doubt; but I think that persons in the trade will find it tolerably easy. If properly executed, the work will be regular and smooth—not "gouty," as it sometimes appears when done by a careless person, but firm and compact. This kind of weft, or, indeed, any kind of weft, can be made coarse or fine, according to the purpose for which it is intended; but however thick or thin it may be, the work must be uniform and evenly set.

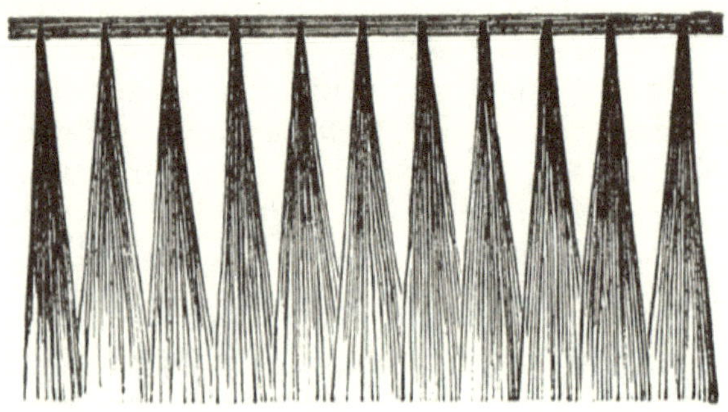

Fig. 3.

"Twice In," or Front Weft (Fig. 3), somewhat resembles, when the silks are open, the letter M, and to do this properly the weaving has to be increased so as to keep the wefts farther apart, and withal, firm. Should the weft be loosely done, it will be unpleasant to sew up, and the job when completed is not likely to be durable or satisfactory.

Follow the directions previously given, until you come to "drawing it through 3 and 2 again." Having done this, continue as follows:—Pass it under 1 and 2, draw it through 3 and 2, turn it over the top, and end as before by bringing the roots through (or between) the lower silks.

This kind of weft can be executed by an expert both rapidly and well, but perhaps a yard an hour would be considered satisfactory, especially if it were found perfect when completed.

"Thrice In," Crop, or Wig Weft, should be very finely made, taking about six or eight hairs at a time to make a weft, depending of course on the quality of the hair used. Each weft should be tolerably wide apart, and firmly woven, if durability in a wig be required. When it is remembered that twenty or thirty yards are wanted in the manufacture of a gentleman's wig, my reason for saying that the wefts should be fine and well-set must be apparent, for were it otherwise, the article would be heavy and uncomfortable to the wearer. Lightness ought never to be lost sight of in matters of this description, neither should strength and durability be forgotten. Bearing these instructions in mind then, proceed as though you were going to make "Front weft" but giving the hair a turn or two more, and end by drawing the roots through between the lower silks. Nimble fingers can do this kind of weft in a very expeditious manner, and I have heard of regular weavers making about three yards of wig weft in an hour—so much for constant practice.

"Fly" weft, for top rows, lies very close and compact; the roots fly apart or separate from the other portion of the hair, and they are either to be removed by the scissors, or else pressed downwards with hot pinching-irons previous to cutting down the weft. Indeed, it would be advantageous to "pinch" all pieces of close weft, where flatness and neatness are desired. "Fly" weft covers work very nicely; it should always be finely done and pushed up close. It is made the same way as "once in," but with this exception, namely,—instead of drawing the roots "between the two lower silks" at the last movement, draw them again through the top ones. The roots will stand out or "fly" in an upward direction, and it may be necessary to use a "jockey." By preference, press the roots with hot irons instead of cutting them off, for a weft or two might come out in wear, and then, to say the least, it would look unsightly, and jeopardise the rest.

I shall have occasion to refer again to weaving, but enough has been said for the present.

"Ringlet bunches" applies chiefly to side curls made of ringlet hair, irrespective of the length of hair, or quantity. They can be sewn up close, showing a back as well as front; with all the weft concealed except that upon the top, or in diamond shaped-openings, as shown in Fig. 4.

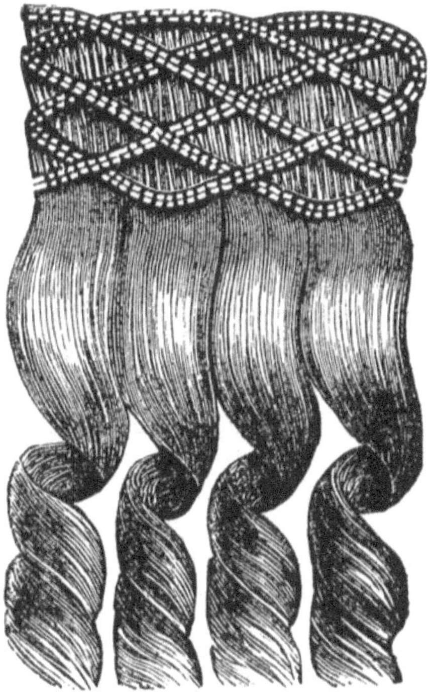

Fig. 4.

The illustration represents one of a pair of "bunches" made with three-quarters of an ounce of fourteen-inch ringlet hair. To begin then: separate the hair, putting the curls which turn one way together, and do the same with the others. All curls which come from the hair-merchant turn both right and left—two ringlets to one lock of hair. In making up either, always remember that the curls should be so arranged as to "turn to the face," for if you do not attend to this at the beginning, the curl is not likely to form or droop properly, and there will most likely be a "cramp" necessitating its being rolled up again and heat applied. With new work this is best avoided, and by attention to the instructions the curls will be made "right and left" as they always ought to be. Next weigh the hair, putting an equal quantity into each scale. Tie up each lot; card it properly, and it will assume almost of itself, or with a very little help, a curl. Now you have two curls, tied at the roots, and inclining one to the right and the other to the left. Take one of them, place it in the brushes, and weave (*see* Fig. 2); when woven, comb it out carefully while on the frame, and form several ringlets all turning the same way. Cut the middle silk six or eight inches from the weft, tie it to the others, and fasten off securely. Now weave the other tress, making the weft to correspond, so as to resemble the first piece as much as possible, in every respect; the curls of course being all turned in a reverse direction. Fasten off and cut down as before. You have now the weft for a pair of curls, and it has to be sewn up. Take one of the pieces, and double it, pressing the fold with your thumb and finger so as to temporarily mark it. This will give the centre of the piece. Fold one of these halves into three (so as to get at the width to make them) and then let the top one go loose. You are now holding between the thumb and finger of the left hand two rows of weft. Sew the end to the adjoining row with silk specially made for trade use, and the stitches are all to be in one spot. Then sew at a proper distance again and again in the same manner, and this will complete the two lower rows of weft. Take up another row, so arranging as to bring the stitches exactly in the centre of the "diamond" until you get to the end of that row. Do the same with any other rows until completed. Pull into form with the thumb and finger; slightly damp the weft, and press into shape with warm pinching-irons. The other bunch, of course, is to be made to match. If intended for stock they had better be attached with the needle and silk, so as to keep the "bunches" together, otherwise they will get mixed and cause confusion.

I must here observe that the experienced eye will notice a slight difference between the letterpress description and the illustration. I did not perceive the error until too late, but for the sake of accuracy I think it necessary to draw attention to it. The weft as shown in the engraving passes from bottom to top and *vice versâ*, whereas in the description it is in rows—one above the other. The artist has in the main given the design correctly enough, but the *modus operandi* by which it is produced is not so clearly indicated as I would desire.

Sometimes the weft is sewn up close, and that is more particularly the case when space is taken into consideration. If the work has to cover a rather large surface, it is best to sew it up in diamond shapes, but if it is to be condensed, then the wefts should be fine, close, and made up in as compact a manner as possible. Take, for instance, another lot of hair, the same in weight and length as the preceding. Observe the instructions given concerning its division, and weave as before. Measure off as previously described, and supposing that you allow for six rows of weft, proceed as follows:—Fold back one over and above the other, and securely stitch the end by way of a commencement. Push the needle *towards* you through the centre of the lower row of weft, and *from* you through the upper row of weft. Avoid sewing "over and over." Keep all the stitches small, and the sewing-silk is not to be doubled. Having worked in this way from end to end, take another row of weft, and put in position over the lower row. Sew it as before described, and so on until the whole is completed. The weft will be seen at the back, occupying, when made up, about half the depth required in Fig. 4. The worker must be particular in keeping the rows of weft straight and flat, which he can easily do with attention and the proper use of his thumb and finger. I say "finger," because curled hair should never be held in the hand, for the warmth of the hand is likely to cramp or weaken the curl. Comb out, press, and dress as before described. Another way, so as to hide the weft altogether, excepting the top row, can be done when required. Take a similar lot of hair, and weave it. Commence sewing up as before, and when the two rows are done, instead of turning the weft backwards and forwards so as to show the work, turn it round and round in order to conceal it, still sewing-up flat as previously described.

Tufts of hair are side pieces or curls, and the weft is wound round a side comb instead of being sewn upon it, as will presently be mentioned. The word "tuft" may be applied to almost any small piece of *postiche* hair, whether it be upon a comb or a hair-pin, as "pin-curls" are made. I have seldom heard the designation of "tuft" applied to any piece of hair in a London shop, though I have known it to be common in some parts of the country, therefore it may be taken to be a provincial more than a common term used in the trade. Tufts, then, can be made of any length and thickness, depending entirely upon the use for which they are intended. Two tufts, *i.e.*, two bunches of lightly-formed ringlet curls, might be employed in a lady's coiffure with considerable advantage. They could be placed behind the ears, or so arranged near the tie (or knot) as to form a pretty *cache-peigne*, while "pin-curls" could be put wherever fancy might direct. To make the tufts, take fine weft, and side combs with rather open teeth. Arrange both hair and combs for the right and left sides. Fasten the weft to that part of the comb which is intended to go nearest the forehead, and let the hair hang towards the face. Having secured the weft with needle and silk, cut the silk off, leaving only the weft upon the comb. Then commence winding up the weft around the back of the comb, keeping it firm, and allowing one row of weft to go between each tooth. Each layer of weft conceals that which precedes it, and the weft should all be used up before reaching the top. About two-thirds of the back of the comb might be covered, and when this is reached finish off with the needle. The hair will be found in a rather rough condition, but that does not much signify to a patient workman. It will be necessary to get some one to hold it (which must be done with both hands, to prevent any undue strain upon the comb) while you disentangle the hair, turning the curl over the work on the back of the comb. Put it on a block, press the work with warm irons, and dress out in the form required. "Pin-curls" are simply pieces of weft of short curled hair, and made up after the manner just described.

Fig. 5.

Curls on combs, when nicely made, are very effective, being intended to wear at the sides. Tortoise-shell combs should be used, rather open teeth, and "grailed," of a pliable quality, and those known in the trade as "rights" and "lefts" I have always found to be the best for this kind of work. Divide, and prepare the hair as in the previous instances. Weave one row of "fly weft" out of each piece, and this should be as long as the fine teeth of the comb extend. Begin and finish this weft in a secure manner, and let each piece be distinct from the other. Pinch, and cut down. Weave the other two pieces in the ordinary way, beginning and finishing off each one separately. Comb out, pinch, and cut down. You have now four distinct pieces of weft, a long and a short, fine piece for each comb. Take the longest piece of weft and fold it into two, three, or four lengths (as the case may be), each length being at least a quarter of an inch shorter than the fine-toothed part of the comb. Sew it up close, because, in this instance, the work has to be "condensed." You cannot make the weft too flat, and, of course, the weft is to lie upon the comb. Comb out and pinch. Take up the comb, say, for the right side, and the "fly" weft for that side also. Hold the curls drooping in your left hand, and the comb (the concave part uppermost) in your right. Pass the teeth of the comb through the hair nearest the weft, and then pull it gently into its place. Take your needle and silk and, as needle-women say, "fasten on." This part of the job is to be done carefully, taking one stitch to each tooth (the weft being down towards the points), the reason for this is to avoid breaking the teeth. Bear in mind to make the stitches loose, otherwise the weft will not fit into its right position close to the top of the comb; but if they are too slack the work will not keep in its place at all. This important point, like many others, can only be gained by observation and practice. The "fly" weft, remember, is in the concave or hollow part of the comb, while the "twice in" weft is to be on the convex, or upper part. Take this part, then and put it into its place. Incline it towards the points to allow the needle to pass through easily. Fasten on, and make a stitch to every tooth as before. Push it up close to the "top" row, and with two or three small stitches taken at random connect the whole together. Pursue the same plan with respect to the one intended for the opposite side, when, of course, they will form a pair. Comb out, press with *curling* irons, and arrange. I may say, *inter alia*, that while the hair is in a rough, dishevelled state, a little—only a little—of the very best olive oil, nicely perfumed, should be applied. It facilitates the action of the comb, renders the hair easier to dress, and adds a gloss to it which, if not overdone, heightens the effect. Pomade of any kind should not be used to curled, or, indeed, to any kind of "false" hair. My reason for saying so is, that it tends to "clog" the hair, does not impart such a fine gloss, and causes it sooner to become sticky.

"Alexandra curls" form a very pretty addition to the coiffure. The curl or curls are occasionally made with a portion of the back hair set apart for the purpose, but it sometimes happens that there is not sufficient in quantity or length, or that it will not retain the curl, and then the necessity arises for artificial aid. The long ringlet curls here represented, were named after Her Royal Highness the Princess of Wales, and for a great length of time remained in fashion. Sometimes two or more are worn, and in that case, they would be so disposed as to fall in front and behind the shoulder. They add a charm to the coiffure, and impart a nice finish to the whole. They are made as follows:—Take three-quarters of an ounce of eighteen-inch hair, or an ounce of twenty-inch hair, and so on in proportion according to the length. The hair must be specially prepared for the purpose, otherwise the curl will be too heavy, and "break" towards the top. To prepare the hair for Alexandra curls take, say, half an ounce of twenty-inch, and a like quantity of twelve-inch hair, curled. Card and mix the two lengths together, which, if properly done, will form a long curl, and light at the bottom as it should be. But Messrs. R. Hovenden and Sons, as well as other hair merchants, keep "taper curled hair for Alexandra curls" in stock, of divers lengths and shades of colour, and it is much better to obtain the hair already manipulated, than to do it oneself. The mode of making these curls is similar to that adopted for making hair-twists, and fully described in the next chapter. Having been sewn up, the hair must be carefully combed out, pinched at the top where the work is, and dressed. A long stick, termed a "curlstick," is generally used for the latter purpose; the hair being adroitly put round it (commencing at the top, not at the bottom) and brushed; the stick is then withdrawn and the curls remain as shown on the previous page.

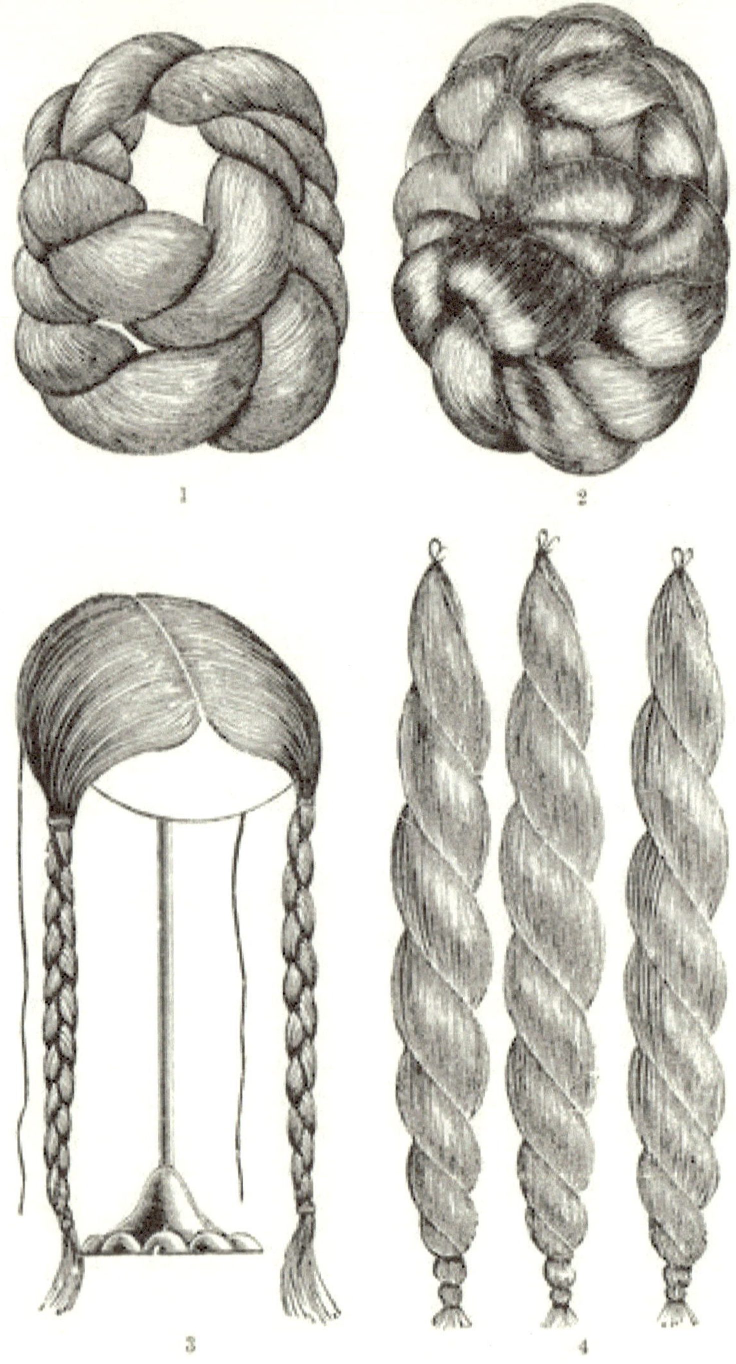

1. Spanish Coil Chignon. 2. Beatrice Chignon. 3. Straight Hair Bandeau.
4. Cable Twists, for making the Spanish Coil Chignon, &c.

CHAPTER VI.

Making Twists, "Tails," or Switches—Back and Side Plaits—Chignon *Universel*—The Zephyr Coiffure—Semi-waved Curled Chignon—A Novel Chignon—Of Chignons in general.

Twists, "Tails" or Switches are made first into sections or stems, and two, three, four, or five, are required to form a complete twist, or "tail." The word "tail" is used more as a trade term than anything else, although I have seen it written upon tickets attached to long pieces of hair, exposed for sale in hairdressers' shop-windows. It is not by any means an elegant way to indicate the article, and *"torsade"* or "twist," is, to my thinking, preferable. The number of stems employed is, generally, three, and they may be long or short, according to the length of hair; the purpose for which the article is designed; and last, but not least, the price. And here, again, the price, as well as the style of manufacture, admits of great variety. A twist can be made to sell for pounds, or shillings, according to the colour, length, thickness, quality, and workmanship. These are matters with which persons engaged in the trade are well acquainted, and I need not further refer to them.

Here is the method of making a twist. Take two ounces of twenty-inch straight hair, and divide into three parts, but one part is to be thicker than either of the other two, so as to allow for a top row, in addition, being made from it. Having done this, tie each lot, temporarily, so as to keep it intact. Fix the weaving frame, and three silks, as on previous occasions. Put the thickest portion into the brushes, and weave a very fine top row of "once-in" weft, about three and a-half inches in length. This is not to be cut down, but go on weaving the remaining portion of the tress of hair; the only difference being that it is to be coarser. The weaving should be graduated, as it were, so as to avoid an abrupt thickness of the weft, for it would, doubtless, spoil the appearance of the work. Plait up in three, and twist the weft round the weaving peg. Leave a space of about four or five inches, and then resume. Commence with a very fine weft, and weave it in the usual manner, taking care to secure it firmly to the silks by a little extra-close weaving. There is a special way of doing this which an expert can easily show, but it is difficult here to describe. Another way of proceeding is to press the first portion with warm irons, cut down, and then begin again, of course without making another top row. Weave the third and remaining tress in the same way, and the work then is ready for sewing up.

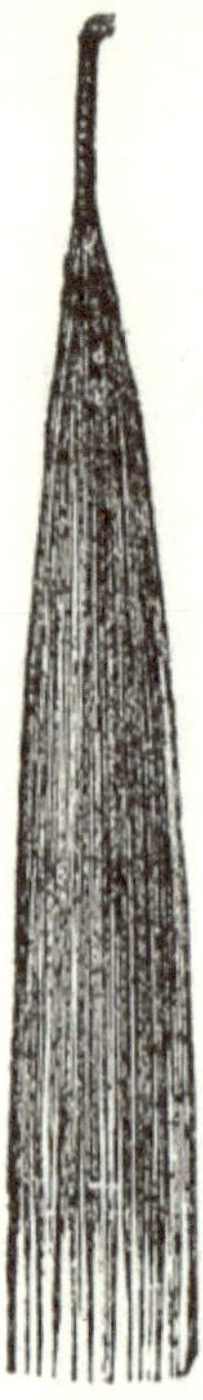

Fig. 6.

To sew up, take a rather short but plain weaving peg, and bore a hole in it about five or six inches from the top. Through this hole pass a stout wire, bend it down to keep it in its place, and form a hook at the bottom; turn the other part of the wire in a corresponding direction, but leaving a piece standing out to form a handle. If this is designed properly, it can easily be turned round and round without becoming detached from its position. Take a piece of black tape, Russian cord, or some other suitable material, about the length of the weft; tie a knot at top and fix it to the wire hook. Commence about an inch from the bottom, by sewing the thick end of the weft to the lower part, and having done so, break off the silk. Begin, then, turning the handle of the wire above described; this will cause the tape or cord to twist, and when sufficiently twisted, it will be proper to roll the weft upon it. Having done so for a little distance, turn the wire again, so as to keep it firm; continue this till the end of the weft is reached, and then fasten off. (See the accompanying illustration of one of the stems, Fig 6.)

It will be necessary to observe that each row of weft should lie close to and above the preceding row, and when there is much weft to be rolled or twisted up it ought to be stitched in several places. Now, having completely made two of the stems, make the third one, *i.e.*, the one with the top row attached. Sew this up as before instructed until you come to the top row, when stop. Take the other two stems, and place the free ends of the tape, cord, or whatever may be the material used, with that which you are now working, and stitch them all together. Having done so, begin sewing the top row, neatly, and well, but having started it, take sufficient Russian cord to make a loop, put it in its place, cover all with the top row, and finish off securely. Each stem is to be pinched separately, and pinched again when completed. (Fig. 7.)

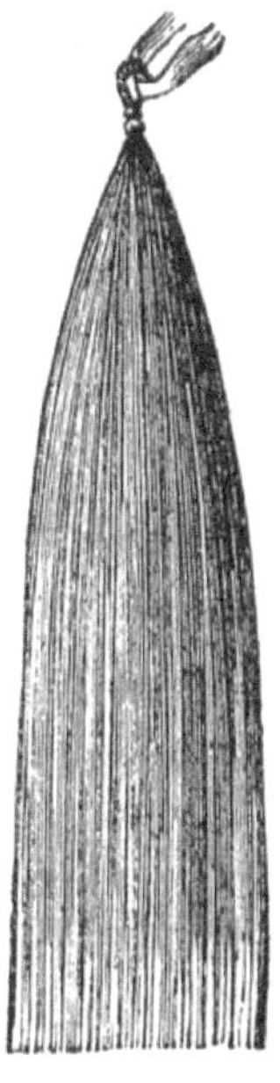

Fig. 7.

These twists are exceedingly useful, and if well-made, with hair of good quality and length, they can be applied to a number of purposes in connection with the coiffure. They may be twisted up with the back hair, made into a plait or plaits, used as a solid twist or a light *torsade* for a coronet, or back hair dressing. Speaking of a *torsade*, the following instructions, taken from "Lessons in Hairdressing," will doubtless prove acceptable. That which I am about to describe is known by the names of *Torsade Dondel, Torsade Repoussée, Torsade Gouffrée*. It is made "with a long thin strand of hair, and is hollow when completed; consequently, where lightness is required, two or three of these may be introduced with charming effect. Proceed to make it in the following manner:—Take a piece of hair from twenty-four to thirty inches long, and separate a thin strand, which afterwards serves as a 'draw.' This put on one side till wanted. Divide the hair into two equal parts, and friz well upon the inner side, at the same time spreading out the hair so as to make it wide and flat. It may then be compared (for further illustrating my instructions) to a long and somewhat wide strip of cardboard. Hold the end in your left hand, and turn upon the thumb of the right hand, which, for the purpose, should be placed near to the top, or roots. Having given it a bend, it then forms a 'hollow,' which is to be so twisted upon itself, and in a spiral direction to the end. Then either pin down temporarily or get the lady to hold it. Proceed in the same manner with the second portion. Having done so, take one end in each hand and twist both together, being particular to pass that held by the left hand over that held by the right. Take then the little strand of hair, and pass it round the *torsade* in such a manner that it falls into every second space. Hold the end firmly, and push up the frizzed twist; fasten off, and place in position."

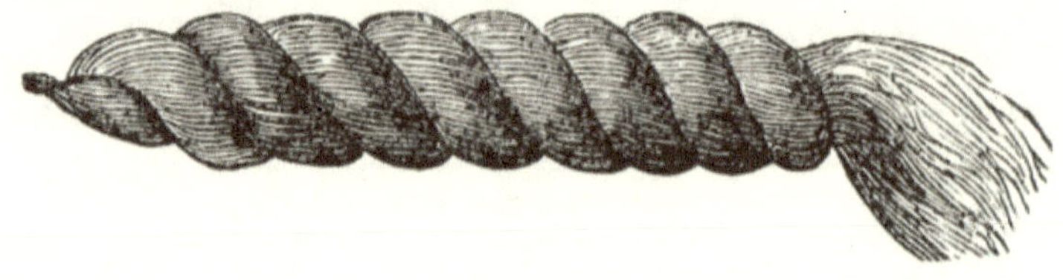

Fig. 8.

It will be seen that when neatly done the whole forms a hollow and "puffed up" twist, light in construction, full in appearance, and very suitable for a coronet or as an embellishment to the chignon.

In the hairdressing business there are innumerable changes of fashion, while the various requirements of different individuals continually make demands upon the practical knowledge of those who carry on the trade. Some articles that I have spoken of, and others to which I shall have occasion to refer, are "not in fashion," but there is an occasional demand for something or another that would puzzle many who profess to know how to make almost everything. It is the duty of a hairdresser to assist nature in matters appertaining to the *chevelure*, for thin locks have to be supplemented by artificial aid, and bald heads not unfrequently require to be covered. It is not at all times pride and vanity that causes people to resort to the use of "false hair," as it is termed, any more than it is pride and vanity which *compels* some folk to use spectacles, wear false teeth, or have recourse to surgical mechanicians for their especial aid and comfort. I could laugh at the remarks occasionally given expression to, for "goody-goody" people seem inclined to condemn in others that which they can dispense with themselves.

To resume. A back plait with a flat top can be made from any quantity or length of hair. It may be wide or narrow as circumstances require, and although the twist before described is in general requisition, yet there are occasions when a flat top is most convenient and suitable. Take half-an-ounce of twenty-inch hair, and two ounces of eighteen. Close, or "once in" weft, throughout. Weave the long hair moderately fine for the top row, or rows, and the eighteen-inch hair should be woven rather coarse, but uniform from beginning to end. There should not be a "break," for all the weft must be in one piece. Pinch, temporarily plait in "threes," and cut down. Decide upon the width the plait is to be made, and sew up firm and regular.

Side Plaits are made with sixteen or eighteen inch hair, after the manner of closely-sewn ringlet bunches; two or three loops are attached to each bunch through which a piece of wide galloon or ribbon is passed. This serves to fasten them to the head, and as they are made to slide, the width apart can be adjusted according to the discretion of the wearer. I have also made side plaits on combs, after the method adopted for making curls on combs, leaving the ends of the plaits to be fixed by the wearer, or by "tacking" them to the combs after being plaited. The ends of these side plaits should be securely fastened by means of black thread, and the whole neatly covered with a piece of ribbon.

Concerning the plaiting of hair, the reader is referred to "Lessons in Hair-dressing," wherein copious instructions are given.

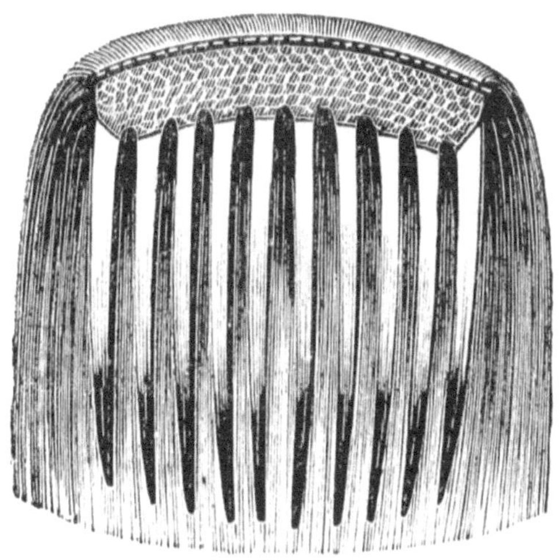

Fig. 9.

The "Chignon Universel," as it is called, is a clever arrangement for making good a deficiency in the back hair; it is most convenient, and unmistakably "defies detection." To be made with smooth hair on the top, with the underneath hair either *créolé*, or plain. If fulness be desired the former plan is most expedient, or else long frizzettes should be introduced. But much depends upon the length and thickness of the hair and the way it is going to be arranged. To manufacture the *Chignon Universel* proceed as follows:—Take half an ounce of twenty-two inch hair, and having previously selected a comb, weave sufficient "fly" weft to make a top row, pinch, securely fasten off, and cut down. Then take two ounces of twenty-inch hair, which is to be woven rather coarse, and I need scarcely add, close, or "once in" weft; the object being to get as much hair as possible into the smallest compass. Sew up as though you were going to make an ordinary back plait according to the instructions previously given. Pinch, and make it as flat as you can. Cover the top of the comb with a piece of strong net, such as is used in wig-making, and do all the sewing on the front part of it, so that when finished it shall present a neat appearance, as shown in the illustration.[5] Securely stitch the piece made with the twenty-inch hair to the net, at the top part of the comb, and in such a way that it lies flat. Then take the piece of "fly" weft, and (putting the roots underneath) sew it on the top, so as to cover all. Press, and comb out the hair.

---

[5] See Fig. 9.

When completed, the work ought to look as compact and pretty as it does in the wood-cut annexed.

Ability comes with practice, and as I am writing for the benefit of those who desire to improve, I would just hint that they need not be afraid of doing their work *too well*. At the outset inferior productions might reasonably be expected, but, as the apprentice or improver advances, better work should be forthcoming. There is an old saying that "practice makes perfect," and that is exemplified in numberless instances every day.

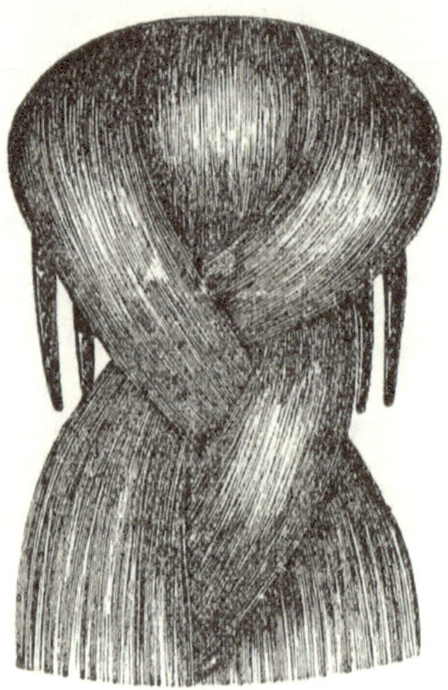

Fig. 10.

Some few years ago several of the leading hairdressers met together, by arrangement, and discussed the necessity which then existed for the introduction of a new style of coiffure. The once-fashionable chignon, with its accompanying plaits and twists had disappeared, and the coiffeur's art began to decline in consequence. Besides, ladies complained of the meagre fashion which succeeded the more elaborate style of hairdressing, and a change, for more reasons than one, was considered necessary. I need not pause here to discuss the importance of the coiffure, or the pleasing effect which is produced when the hair is arranged in harmony with the features. All ladies' coiffeurs are well aware of it, and at the meeting in question it was decided to introduce something new and of almost universal application in reference to ladies' hairdressing. But the time was not sufficiently ripe for a change—the little knot and the fringed brow had taken too great a hold of the popular fancy. However the innovation was of a tasteful and serviceable character, and in expert hands could be made to assume a number of charming designs.

It was called "The Zephyr Coiffure," and is made as follows:—Take some tapered curled hair from sixteen to twenty inches in length, and about an ounce and a quarter in weight. Weaken the curl to within six inches of the points, and sew up on three separate pieces of galloon or net, about a quarter of an inch wide, keeping it flat and soft. The stems may be four or five inches in length, or longer, according to circumstances, while another description is made of a lesser quantity of hair, shorter in proportion, and sewn up in the usual way of making twists or "tails." (See accompanying illustrations.)

The first pieces described can be arranged in puffs, undulations, *rouleaux*, knots, or twists, but those made upon the last-named principle are more suited for plaits, but leaving the ends curled.

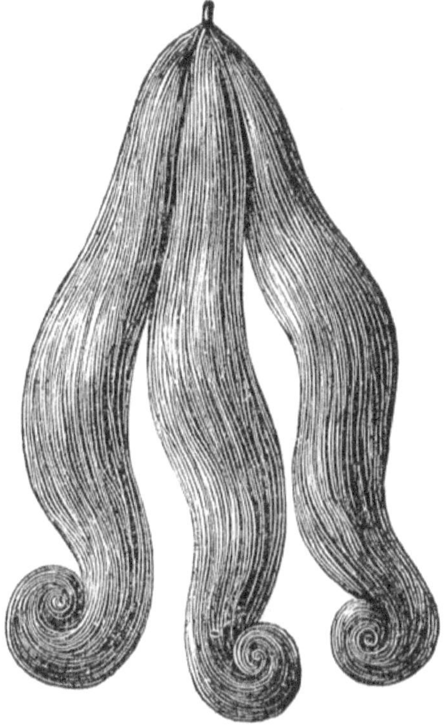

Fig. 11.

The experienced coiffeur will see at a glance what can be done when these additions are introduced. With the lady's own *chevelure*, and the use of two or more of these pieces of hair, a dressing can be devised at once light and elegant, high on the head as with a long coronet, by inserting the stems one into the other and concealing the loops, or low on the neck with tight or fluffy curls. Again, the stems can be incorporated with the back hair, and the curled ends arranged over and upon the forehead. Should the head of hair be of a poor description, through its being short and thin, then three, or at most four, of these tresses will probably be required. The following headdress has been executed to give the reader some idea of the adaptability of these pretty additions to almost any style of hairdressing, while the advantages to be derived from the curled ends may readily be discerned.

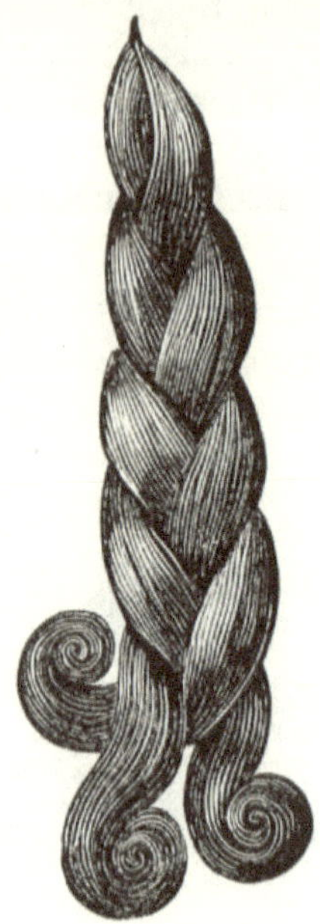

Fig. 12.

In presenting this description of the Zephyr Coiffure, I would remark that not one, but at least twenty different styles can be executed with the help of these necessary adjuncts, and, further, the chignon can be made large or small according to the taste or requirements of the wearer, as can easily be imagined.

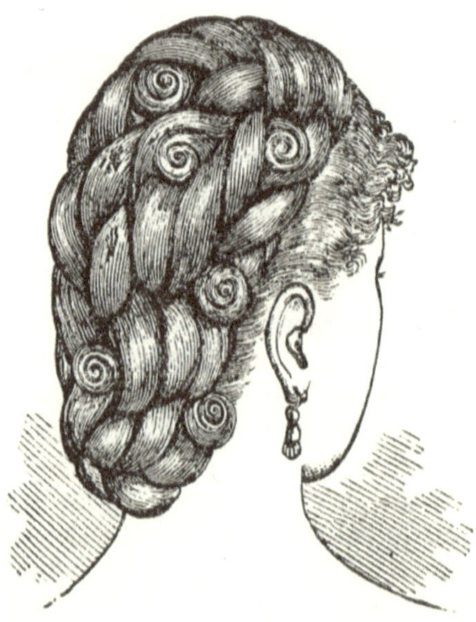

Fig. 13.

While speaking of taper-curled hair, I am reminded of a semi-waved curled chignon which is light in construction and produces a very pretty effect. Of course it can be made either large or small, thick or thin, with longer or shorter hair, and a practised hand will see at a glance its general utility. This *cache-peigne* can be worn with a comb, or embellished with flowers, and, moreover, it presents a most natural appearance. (See Fig. 14.)

Fig. 14.

To make the chignon, take about 3½ ozs. of taper ringlet hair, a part of which is to be twelve inches, another part fourteen, and so on up to the longest, which should be about twenty inches. Instead of weaving upon three silks in the usual manner, fine wire is to be substituted for the centre one. Let the weft be very good, and sew up into a diamond-shaped foundation. (Reference to Chapter V. will show what is meant.) With this quantity of hair the mount should be, when completed, about four inches wide and seven inches long. The weft required is about three yards, and must be so arranged that the shorter hair is kept at the top, while the longest comes to the bottom. To make the wavings, undo the curl a little here and there and friz underneath, or it can be weakened by means of a warm iron. Another *cache-peigne* I have made on a similar principle, but very much lighter, and, with proper dressing, it appears to be nearly as full. Take ¾ oz. or 1 oz. of taper ringlet hair, twelve, sixteen and twenty inches long. Weave and sew up as before directed. In dressing, each curl should be very carefully frizzed in the inside, and disposed *without* the aid of the curl-stick, if possible. By adopting this method, the curls will be very thin and light, and obtain, through frizzing, all the fulness required.

A novel chignon was designed, some time ago, by Mr. Joseph Kubelka (Vienna), which consists of the ingenious combination of two ordinary "tails" or "twists," and is worthy of reproduction here.

Its formation will be seen at a glance,[6] and the method of arrangement is first made upon the hand (the tops being held by some person, or else temporarily fixed to a table), and a "bodkin" must be employed in working the design. This bodkin can be made of tortoise-shell, ivory, or bone, but it must have an opening sufficiently large to encircle the free ends of the hair. (The illustration given below indicates very clearly how the plait is to be made.)

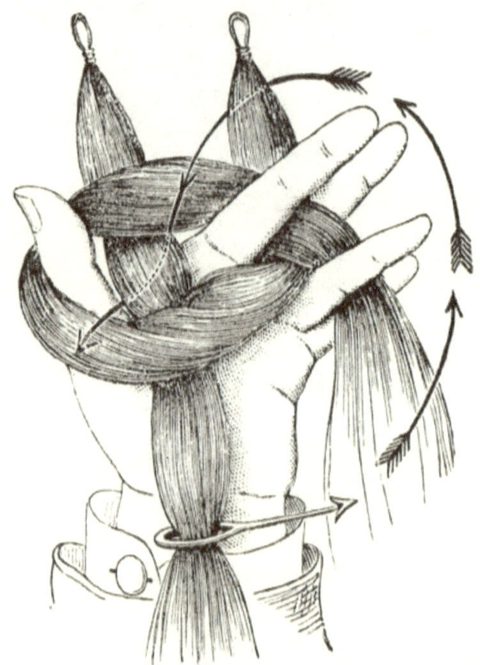

Fig. 15.

By means of this contrivance the hair is drawn through spaces easily made by the fingers, and, as can readily be discerned, the plaited chignon well holds itself together. The final disposition of the ends must be completed upon the head, when they (as well as the natural hair) should be made into *rouleaux*, etc., as may be found most convenient and tasteful. Where lightness has to be considered, perhaps two well-covered inserted stems might take the place of a quantity of hair—a hint which is not likely to be overlooked by clever hairdressers.

---

[6] Fig. 16.

Fig. 16.

Probably, at this juncture, some remarks on chignons in general will not be thought out of place. Chignons may be considered as "old as the hills," for the word simply means as I interpret it—a back hair dressing without reference to any particular shape. Were I to designate the mere "knot" at the back of the head a chignon, perhaps my meaning would not be clearly understood, but it is in reality as much a chignon as the most elaborate one could be. In the ordinary acceptation of the word, however, a fanciful style of dressing the back hair is meant, and "Board-work" would not be complete without special allusion being made to chignons, seeing that their manufacture a few years ago gave employment to thousands of people of both sexes.

M. Alphonse Bouchard, writing in THE HAIRDRESSER'S CHRONICLE on the subject of "False Hair," says that "the compilers of the General Catalogue of the Universal Exhibition, 1867, have given us figures, which it would be very difficult to check; but they, no doubt, used the same sources which I have had recourse to, and to prove the exactness and authority of this essay, I shall quote a few data.

"This official document reports as follows:—The manufacture of hair is to-day of very great importance. Paris is the place where the hair is well prepared, and where the headdresses arrive at the highest degree of perfection. The price of raw hair, says this catalogue, is about 50 francs on an average per kilo. It was 65 francs in 1865; and it is said to have been sold even at 100 francs. The price of prepared hair is 140 francs the kilo. The price of *postiches* is about 40 francs apiece; the prices of the fashionable coiffures, called chignons, range from 15 francs to 200 francs, and even as far as 500 francs apiece. In France about 70,000 kilos. of cut hair are sold. Of this quantity 40,000 kilos. are French, and 20,000 kilos. are imported from Italy, Belgium, Germany and other countries. 8,000 kilos. are collected in the workshops and other places; this is called 'waste.' America, England and Prussia buy 30,000 kilos. of hair of us; 25,000 kilos. are used in France in the manufacture of *postiches*; and about 13,000 kilos. are exported to different countries. Marseilles is next to Paris in importance for the hair trade. M. Joseph Mathieu has given us some curious details on the hair trade in Marseilles. He tells us, that the statutes of the wig-makers of Marseilles date from 1696. Their number was for a long time limited to twenty. In 1760, the master-wigmakers of Marseilles, seeing that a large number of ladies' hairdressers established themselves in that city, commenced an action against them. But a decree of the 20th June, 1761, rejected these pretensions, and gave full and entire freedom to the ladies' hairdressers to exercise their calling.

"In 1789, the number of hairdressers and ladies' hairdressers of Marseilles was considerable. It is well known how complicated the headdresses of that period were, and according to the records of that time, Marseilles was one of the first cities in France for elegance and good taste.

"After the Revolution the number of hairdressers increased gradually, but it is more especially during the last ten years that this increase has been mostly noticed, and to-day we have at Marseilles 397 coiffeurs.

"Four houses, employing about forty workmen, hold the monopoly of the hair trade. The trade has increased fourfold during the last thirty years. The houses in the trade receive together annually 6,000 kilos. of hair, from the Tyrol, Bohemia, Dalmatia and Italy. Having been worked, 3,000 kilos. of this quantity is sent to the provinces and to foreign countries, and 3,000 kilos. remain for town consumption.

"It is estimated that of these, 500 kilos. are used for men's wigs, and 2,500 kilos. for *postiches* for women. The *postiches*, chignons, *cache-folies* and false plaits are employed to such an extent, that there are at Marseilles actually 75,000 women, or the whole grown-up female population, who wear false hair. This observation applies equally to Paris and to some large towns abroad. All coiffeurs at Marseilles trade in chignons more or less, and their annual production of this article amounts to 55,000. Of these, 30,000 are sent to the provinces, and 25,000 are sold in the city and its suburbs.

"Corresponding with the advance of education in France, the difficulty to find young countrywomen who are ready to part with their *chevelure* increases. Nowadays it requires a sum of money to induce a girl to undergo the ordeal of the cutter's scissors; consequently we have been obliged to go elsewhere in search of this article, principally to Germany, Austria, Italy, and more particularly to Sicily, the Neapolitan provinces, and the former Papal states. The large religious communities of women furnish also great quantities of hair. In certain Catholic countries the hair of the novice who enters a religious order is sold for the benefit of the convent where the vow is taken, and those beautiful tresses, sacrificed at the foot of the altar by virgins who renounce the world, return to it again other heads to adorn. The Italian hair is imported into France viâ Marseilles, and the figure of this importation reached in 1865 17,367 kilos.

*   *   *   *   *

1. Coiled Chignon, measuring thirty-six inches, or more, when undone.
2. Pair of side Frizzetts. 3. Seven Strand Double Plait. 4. Marguerite
Plait: This can be plaited in 4, 5, 6, or 7 strands, as may be decided upon.
5. Bertha Frizzett (set of three), for Plaited Chignon: The stems are
made with straight hair inserted, of medium thickness, and seventeen
inches in length.

"In 1830, the value of raw and manufactured hair exported from France amounted to 104,488 francs; in 1865 it had increased to 1,206,605 francs. Numbers of people at Paris, at Marseilles, and in other large towns, have realised fortunes in the hair trade. Let us mention one house in the Palais Royal quarter which, in 1868, did business to the amount of 1,552,000 francs. We may safely say that the French hairdressers sell annually 68,000 kilos. of hair, which, made into plaits, curls, crape, etc., represents a sum of 80,000,000 francs. Let us further mention that another house sold, within sixteen months, in 1871 and 1872, 16,000 chignons, at prices varying from 12 to 70 francs each, but of course there are much more expensive ones sold, chignons of a natural red or golden tinted hair, which is principally imported from Scotland, being the most expensive."[7]

From the foregoing, the reader can learn what the trade *was* a few years ago; but what it *is* now, his every-day experience can answer.

Undoubtedly the manufacture of chignons was a thriving trade so long as it lasted, and we have it on record that of a certain dyed material termed "hair" (which it greatly resembled) "hundreds of thousands of tons" were used in the making of frizzettes, pads, etc.[8]

It would be useless now to enter upon the method of constructing chignons, for their patterns are almost endless; but with inserted stems, or pads, and suitable hair, an ingenious hairdresser ought to be able, after what I have already said, to make several of neat and pretty designs.

---

[7] Concerning French weights, measures, and money, the following information will, doubtless, be useful:—The unit in weights is the gramme. 28 of which go to the English ounce; 1,000 grammes are called a kilogramme, or, shortened, a kilo., equal in weight to 2 lb. 3 oz. 4 drs. English avoirdupois. The unit in measures is the metre, equal in length to 39⅓ inches English. The metre is divided into 1,000 parts, each of which is called a millimetre; 10 millimetres are called a centimetre. The length of a centimetre is rather more than one-third of an inch English, the figure in decimals being 0·39371. One foot English is equal to 304 millimetres, and an inch equals rather more than 25 millimetres. The unit in money is the franc, equal to ninepence-halfpenny English. The franc is divided into one hundred parts, each of which is called a centime; five centimes are called a sou; and a sou is rather less in value than a half-penny.

[8] Donisthorpe *v.* Jowett, 1876; *vide* Law Report in *The Hairdressers' Chronicle*.

CHAPTER VII.

Scalpettes and Fringes; general remarks thereon—Curled and Waved
Fringes—"Water Waves"—Mounting and Making Scalpettes.

Baldness is not by any means confined to the male sex, for females, through illness, *accouchements*, neuralgic pains in the head, constitutional weakness, frequent head-aches, tying the hair improperly, overmuch crimping, and other causes—frequently experience a loss of hair. True, this can easily be concealed by means of headdresses, bows, ribbons, flowers, lace, and so forth, but young and middle-aged ladies do not find it convenient to have recourse to such artifices at all times. Formerly, *bandeaux* and "fronts" were employed to conceal this defective condition of the hair, and they are still in request by elderly people and those whose means are limited. But now, thanks to the ingenuity of ladies' hairdressers, the "scalpette" has been invented, and it may truly be regarded as a veritable work of art. What is a scalpette? As this is comparatively a new word, it will be advisable to dwell for a moment upon its meaning. I therefore consider it to signify *an artificial covering for* concealing *a deficiency of hair*, or to cover *a bald place upon the female head*—but not a wig. Just the same as a "scalp" is an artificial covering for the bald head of a man—but it is not a wig. Assuming, then, that my definition is correct, those of my readers who have much to do with board-work will readily perceive the variable nature of the invention. A scalpette can be made to cover a small space, or the entire top of the head; it can be formed with or without a "fringe;" with or without a parting or partings. It can be manufactured with long straight hair, or short curly hair, or both. It can be "knotted" upon gauze or a "human hair foundation," and made, figuratively speaking, "as light as a feather," or it can be woven, and mounted with net and galloon, which is, doubtless, more durable and less expensive. In short, a scalpette can be adapted to any possible requirement, and that there is a demand for such manufactures at good prices in certain localities, both in town and country, will not, probably, be contradicted.

Speaking of sundry ingenious contrivances for concealing bald patches, and helping thin partings to an improved appearance, the *Queen* newspaper observes that the modes of covering thin partings are various. "First, if the head is very bald at the top, a scalpette of straight hair is added; this comes to a point in front, so that any hairs that may remain on the forehead are seen; the partings of this scalpette are made of hair, and are quite invisible; secondly a scalpette of small curls is laid over the parting; it rests quite flat on the head, and is dressy and becoming; and thirdly, a scalpette of short straight hair, which forms a fringe in front, and mingles with the wearer's own hair at the sides. The mode of concealing a thinness of the hair at the sides is to insert a piece of long hair, mounted on the most invisible of hair partings. This thinness at the sides is generally accompanied by the same at the top of the head; the addition is then made to conceal all together. The wearer's own hair is parted at the side, the addition added and kept in its place by a few hairs brought over, and then the whole dressed together, the added piece being quite imperceptible. Another mode is the scalpette which curls at the top, and has straight hair coming from it on either side. When an entire covering is necessary, there is the invisible topee. These cover the parting with short hair, and are on the principle of a front without either springs or strings."

It will appear, as my work advances, how scalpettes can be manufactured, but a knowledge of mounting and knotting must first be acquired, and the other will follow in due course.

Fringes are of a less difficult character, at least the majority of them, but some of the more elaborate ones must, for the reasons given above, stand over for the present.

Fig. 17.

Here is one[9], however, of simple construction, which is made on a wire foundation. Take half an ounce of six-inch hair in tight Sevigny curls. Adjust the weaving-frame, with a wire (instead of silk) in the centre, as has been before described. Make about fifteen inches of close or "once-in" weft. Comb out the hair carefully, curl up, and securely finish off the weft. Cut down. Fold the weft in three equal portions, and neatly, yet firmly, sew the ends together. Take a piece of watch-spring, one-and-a-half or two inches long, and adapt it to fit the bend of the head. Round off the ends, which is to be done with a small, fine file, or by rubbing the corners on a stone. Protect the ends with a piece of waxed kid, thin leather, or parchment, and then cover the spring with galloon. The galloon should be as narrow as possible, with the ends carefully turned in and stitched; it must also be sewn "over and over" at the sides. Gently hammer to make it as flat as possible; and I need scarcely observe that the stitches in this, and all other work should be small and almost invisible. Having thus prepared the spring, put it in position, namely, in the centre of the mount, the lower end being *inside* the weft, to which it is to be sewn. Sew the top row to the top of the spring, while the centre row of weft is, of course, to be attached to the middle of the spring. Tack the "fringe" on to a

---

[9] Fig. 17.

block, and dress in a number of small curls, as shown in the illustration.

Another way is to take three-quarters of an ounce of short, tight curled hair, and make twenty inches of weft or more. Sew up into four rows and put two springs, each one to be full an inch from the ends. In this case, the springs must not be quite so long as the previous one. Dress out as before.

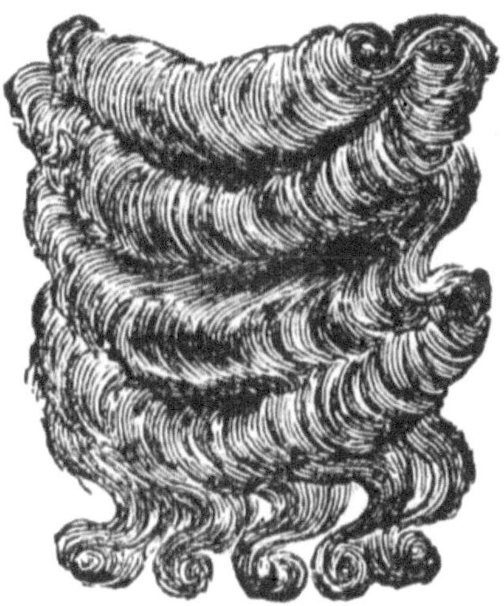

Fig. 18.

Waved Fringes[10] are made of curled hair, perhaps twelve or fourteen inches in length, or more, as occasion may require. The hair is closely woven upon silks, and sewn up in diamond fashion; the width and depth of the same being left to the maker's judgment. This scalpette is very light and lies flat upon the front of the head and forehead. The curl is "broken" by means of damping and a warm iron, and sometimes by a "touch," but only experts can do it properly. Of course, fringes can be made of all sizes and shapes; that matter is generally regulated by the parties concerned, and the price which is to be paid for the article. Some cover the whole front—in that case they would be nine or ten inches long, or even longer, while others are somewhat narrow, extending from front to back; others again have long hair at the sides (only a small portion it is true); but "circumstances alter cases," and the requirements of customers have to be considered.

But the most elegant, vapoury, and artistic "fringes" are, *par excellence*, those which come under the designation of "water waves," so-called, I presume, because water plays an important part in their manufacture. M. Eugene Ménard delivered a very instructive lecture on this subject at the Académie Internationale de Coiffure, in 1884, and perhaps I cannot do better than quote a portion of it. He said, "Any quality of hair, curled or straight, fine or coarse, can be made into water waves, with more or less trouble; but it is certain that fine natural curly hair is the best for that purpose. In default of this hair, which is now very scarce, I should suggest what we call, in French, 'Croquignoles.' This will be found a capital sub-

[10] Fig. 18.

stitute. The next after this, is what is termed in this country, 'tight curl,' and so on, but taking coarse and straight hair for the last, as they never will keep waved. In every instance the hair to be used for water waves, must be well tapered, and as much as possible of a pliable nature. As to blocks, those of porcelain or cardboard, covered with prepared calf's skin or vellum, will be found the most handy and useful for the purpose. Some, I am aware, make use of plain sheet-iron or glass, and yet, after having spent much time over it, they are disappointed at not getting a better result. Why? Because it stands to reason that water waves made in that way, when placed on the head, will not fit any better than the sheet-glass itself, the waves being bound to take the exact shape of that upon which they are made. Therefore, this method will never do, and the idea must be rejected. Others make use of wooden blocks; certainly, when these are new they are quite as good as porcelain, but after they have been put into the oven two or three times—for water waves require to be thoroughly well dried—these blocks become rough and cracked, and consequently, quite useless for that kind of work. Some might, perhaps, object to have the water waves dried in the oven, and would prefer the front of the fire only; if so, my answer would be this: The wood block merely put to the front of the fire might bear the heat once or twice more before being spoilt, but the water waves dried in like manner, would assuredly never last half the time they would if dried in the oven. Experience shows that the oven is the only recipient in which damp hair can be thoroughly well dried, *i.e.*, that the water waves will last with a natural waving appearance.

"Taking for granted that porcelain and cardboard blocks never crack nor become rough by a temperate heat, I will now demonstrate the second great advantage of these two blocks.

"Firstly, I shall deal with the porcelain block, which will be found very suitable for making smooth and perfect water waves, any kind of mounted *postiche*, such as fringes, partings, fronts, scalpettes, etc. Here, I dare say, an apparent difficulty will be found, as neither pins nor points can be driven into porcelain. Therefore, in order to avoid it, I should advise that the block be perforated in four or six different parts, according to the shape of the mounted *postiche* to be dressed, and then to fill the holes with a piece of best quality cork, into which to drive pins and to fix therewith any piece of mounted *postiche*. By so doing the apparent difficulty will be very easily and simply overcome. For instance, place first on the block the scalpette, front, parting, or fringe, in the same way as it is to be placed on the lady's head by whom it is to be worn, and fix it with four or six pins; next, wet the hair right through, and then when thoroughly saturated with water or spirits of wine, brush or comb it down quite flat on the block, and proceed thus: Maintain the mounting or the last wave made, with the medium finger, lift up gently the hair with the thumb of the same hand, and with the comb in the other hand, wet again to the utmost and make the wave, between the two said fingers, according to your wish of the way required. When two or more waves are made, keep the annular finger on the penultimate made wave and support the mounting with the little finger, till you get to the end. Then wet with moderation in upholding the waves, and lift them up again. If necessary, cover the dressed piece of *postiche* with fine muslin or net, so as to see whether the waves are in or out of order; put it into the oven, which must be as hot as the hair can bear without being injured; take it off when thoroughly dried; let it get quite cold; pass the comb through the waves, flatten them with the hand, and then you will get waves as smooth and as natural as can be imagined. I dare say these water waves would cause many an experienced eye to be perplexed in the event of being called upon to make a distinction between them and natural ones. Never divide the hair when the divided parts are intended to make but one wave; at least, do not let it dry in that state, or else the hair will never join together, and the waves—if not entirely disfigured—will be, at least, awry or crooked. On the contrary, wave the whole of the hair at once, even if it is a scalpette—I mean if it is only one wave all round, it is not more difficult, and the waves will be regular. When the hair, however, is over ten or twelve inches long, the first two or three rows of waves might be made separately, but then they must be joined together before proceeding any farther. Another thing to be observed in making water waves is, that they be perfect before drying. When the porcelain block becomes dirty, wash it with soap or soda.

"I shall now proceed with covered cardboard blocks. Vellum or prepared calf's skin, as suggested, is, for the subject I am treating, best adapted to cover cardboard blocks with. These blocks will be found useful for almost any kind of *postiche* to be dressed in *fantaisie* water waves, more especially for light pieces, such as curls on pins, *marteaux* for crown chignons, flat twists, false *nuques relevées*, transformations, loose or unmounted hair, as used by M. Auguste Petit, of Paris, for his well-known "Universal Postiche," etc. The way of proceeding for this kind of water waves is quite different to the former. It will take more time to get the waves made, as it necessitates two distinct preparations. On the first one—although it is very easy to make—will depend the success of the second; and on this second preparation, which requires some little taste to make properly, will depend the success of the waves, whose beauty is to get them methodically hollow. To proceed: Take the *marteau* or any other mounted or unmounted piece of hair—if mounted, the mounting must be straight and not exceeding two inches wide, so as to get the waves perfect from beginning to end—saturate it well, and pin it on the block, then comb it straight, hold it flat between the index and the medium fingers of both hands, and start, either side, by making a kind of zigzag in the same way as you would make waves with curls, varying from one to two inches and a-half wide, according to thickness and size of waves wanted. These zigzags must be very regularly made, and great care taken in order to always have the hair perfectly straight, or in other words, to prevent the underneath hair coming over, and *vice versâ*. Starting from the right side, pull the whole of the piece of hair with the two above-mentioned fingers of the hand; keep the piece of hair loose, and close to the block, between the two same fingers of the left hand, just in the middle of the zigzag; leave off, first, the medium finger of the right hand, elevate it a little, weigh gently on the hair with the index, take this finger off, fix the part made of the zigzag with a pin; proceed in the same manner with the left hand, and go on alternately till you get at the end of the piece of hair to be waved. Curl the extreme point of the hair if thought necessary. Then put it into the oven and let it well dry. Here ends the first preparation.

"Now for the second. When the zigzag piece of hair is quite cold, take off the pins that served to fix it on the block, pass the comb through, friz it underneath, if necessary, place and fix it again on the block, but dry this time, tap slightly over it, fix another pin at each extremity of the intended waves, attach a thin thread or cotton to the first pin, pass that cotton or thread pretty tightly over the zigzag—which will now soon be a wave,—widen this in forming the hollow by the help of the fine teeth of a dressing comb, tighten the thread, stop it at the pin opposite the one from which the thread comes, and so on till the last wave is made. Then damp the dressed piece of *postiche*, put it once more into the oven; let it thoroughly well dry; and when quite cold, take off pins and filament, and you will get some splendid water waves ready to wear. When pins driven into the skin-covering of the block leave a kind of rough bump caused by the heat, pass over it the pressing iron, and it will become flat and smooth again.

Now, concerning the liquid to be used—I am of opinion that warm water, previously boiled with a very little soda in it, is the very best component to wet the hair with for water waves; boiling water and soda, or potash if preferred, having both the property of softening the hair; but, of course, this is only recommended for dark colours. For light ones, suppress the soda, and for grey or white hair, let the boiling water get quite cold, and add to it a very little of Reckitt's blue, so as to prevent the hair from turning of a yellowish tint. To dry this hair it will be also very prudent to cover it with light blue tissue paper. Spirits of wine is also a very good liquid to make use of for water waves; it does not soften the hair so much as the above-stated, but on the other hand, it causes the waves made with it to last much longer. To make use of it, like water, a great quantity is required, more especially when waves are to be made on a porcelain block; therefore, unless a great number of waves are made with it, it would cost very often more than the piece of *postiche* itself. It is more adapted for hair merchants or *coiffeurs posticheurs*. Great care must be taken in using spirits of wine, chiefly when *postiche* dressed with it is drying at the front of the fire. The slightest spark would be enough to spoil it.

Scalpettes and fringes, as I have before indicated, admit of great variety. Indeed, both in make and style of dressing, there is ample scope for the coiffeur to exhibit his skill, and those scalpettes of a fanciful and gossamer-like character are remarkable for taste and ingenuity.

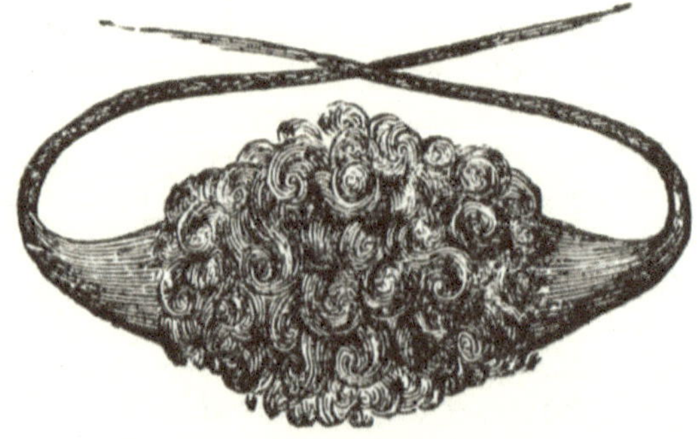

Fig. 19.

To make one as indicated above, with which long straight hair is associated, take ten, twelve or more inches of galloon (according to the size decided upon), double it together, and sew firmly at the ends, leaving, say, a quarter of an inch free. Find the centre of the galloon, tack it by means of "points" to the forehead portion of a clean wig-block, and affix the ends in a similar way; your object being to make a "mount" about three inches deep in the centre, four, five, or six inches long, and tapering off at the sides. The galloon ends, of which I spoke just now, must be at the top, so that when taken off the block only a fine seam is noticeable. Having attended to this, the mount has to be "basted" and formed. The one I am describing is of a diamond shape, and the basting stitches are to be at the bottom, top, and sides. Drive a point into the centre of the block an inch and a half below where you purpose the lower part of the mount to be. Use stout cotton, single, tie a knot at the end of it, and attach to the "point"; take a firm stitch through the galloon and draw it gently down into position. Twist the cotton round and round the "point," finishing with a loop made with the finger; then take one or more similar stitches upon each side terminating in a like way. Give the "point" a tap or two with the hammer, bend it down, and knock the head of it *into* the block. Proceed with the top in a like fashion, and then the ends, or sides. You have now made a step towards "mounting," and that which I have described is not by any means difficult of execution.

It must be borne in mind that I am not addressing myself to novices, but to young men who, at all events, have some knowledge of the trade, and I presume they will not experience much trouble in getting a practical illustration from a friend should they require it. To proceed; take the block in your lap, and commence sewing on the net. Begin on the right-hand side of the inside edge of the bottom galloon, the stitches being moderately close together. Having reached the left-hand corner, turn the block round, and commence sewing in the same manner to the inside edge of the top piece of galloon. While all this is being done pull the net tight, keep it smooth and avoid "puckering," cut away the superfluous net, but—and this is important—the edge of the net which is stitched to the mount ought to well cover two-thirds of the galloon. Now you have both galloon and net upon the block, and the work ought to be strong and secure. A spring, rubbed or filed down, and covered as before described, is to be placed in the centre; but it must not overlap the mount, either at top or bottom.

About half an ounce of short, curled hair (or less, according to the size of the mount) and an equal quantity of sixteen or eighteen inch straight hair will, perhaps, be sufficient; but more can be added if desired. The hair has to be made up into rather fine front-weft or "twice-in." The straight hair weft should also be fine, and equally divided; but the curled hair can be left all in one piece. Sew the straight hair on to the sides first; begin at the point (or end of the mount), and let the rows of weft be firm, regular, and at equal distances from each other. I need scarcely say that the straight hair has to be incorporated with the wearer's own hair when it is dressed, and then two or three hair-pins will keep the "fringe" in place. That portion of the mount to be covered with straight hair will depend upon circumstances, of which you must be the judge. The curled hair has now to be sewn to the mount. "Fasten on securely," as seamstresses would say, and sew along the bottom of the galloon, from right to left, taking about one stitch to every weft. Turn the block, and sew another row along the upper part of the galloon, being careful to cover the free edge of the net, which thus becomes stitched a second time by this operation. The rows of weft are sewn in a like manner until the mount is covered. When turning the weft see that it is done neatly where it joins the straight hair, so that no irregularity or ugly spaces are visible. The weft has now to be pressed (for which a special tool called a "pressing-iron" is used), and the hair properly arranged. Cut the basting stitches, pull them out from the mount, and examine your work. If the stitches are very small, the weft even, the mount a good shape, and the work unmistakably firm and secure, I should pronounce it to be satisfactory; but if there be imperfections in any of these respects, then follow the best advice it is possible to give, and, "Try, try, try again."

Fig. 20.

This design shows a scalpette, intended to cover the top of the head, and, when it is worn, the straight hair should be tied, or twisted in with the natural hair at the back. A covering of this description is very useful when a bald place exists, or there is a thinness of the natural growth of the hair.

In making it, the following instructions should be observed: Upon a clean block, mark with a black lead pencil (in its proper position) the form and size of the mount wanted. Take a piece of galloon and commence by driving a point or two through it, somewhere about the temple. Keep it firm by means of points, as you proceed along the pencilled lines, until both ends of the galloon meet. Cut off, but leave sufficient length to take hold of with the thumb and finger. Pinch together, and with needle and silk sew tight and close, leaving short ends as before. I will suppose that you intend to put on a mount four inches deep, and five inches wide, in shape nearly square, the front (or lower galloon) being drawn down a little. You will have to put basting stitches at the four corners, and also in the centre to make it the desired form. Sew on a piece of galloon extending from left to right, an inch and a-half from the top, one spring in the middle, and others if necessary to keep the corners out. Cover with net, and the mount is complete. You now have an inch and a-half space for the back hair and two and a-half inches space for the front, the joinings taking place upon the piece of galloon affixed for the purpose. Sew on the straight hair first, and then the curled, observing the directions before given. About half an ounce of short curled hair will be sufficient for the one part, and three-quarters of an ounce of sixteen or eighteen-inch hair for the other. Fine weft; press, finish off, and a reference to the illustration[11] will show its arrangement.

A great many articles of this description are "knotted" instead of being woven, and it is simply mentioned here to enable me to say that I shall deal with that part of the subject by-and-bye.

---

[11] Fig. 20.

CHAPTER VIII.

The Changeability of Fashion—Bandeaux, Fronts, and Fillets—Plain
Bandeaux—Waved Bandeaux, with Fringe—To Wave the Hair of
Bandeaux—French (woven) Fronts—French (woven) Fronts, with
Parting—Diamond-shaped and Wing Fronts—Temple-mounted
Fronts—Fillets or Cauls.

Fashion is ever changing, and the fickle goddess does not seem to know her own mind for very long together. And this remark is as applicable to hairdressing as it is to dress, or, indeed, anything else with which the leaders of *ton* have to do. To coiffeurs nothing perhaps is more interesting than a perusal of old illustrated books, and to note the various styles of coiffure. Fifty years ago, when Felix displayed his talent in hairdressing, the front was distinguished by a cluster of curls, made with properly cut and tapered hair of about seven or eight inches in length, and these curls were designated "frizzed," or "French curls." Old hairdressers can remember the "French Fronts," to which I shall merely allude. They were made upon wires, with full and round curls (though done with a thin layer of hair), and the roots as well as the points were woven in together. There would probably be five, six, or seven of these curls upon each side; but for an illustration of them I can only refer the reader to the fashions of bye-gone days. At the period to which I am referring (and long after), it was no uncommon thing to find in hairdressers' shops a large stock of fronts and bands, and though they may never come into general use again, still, those who wish to be proficient in board-work, should learn how to make them. To be well-grounded in the rudiments of any trade is of the greatest importance, for all must have a beginning, and the more skilful work of the clever tradesman will surely follow after.

There used to be a good demand for *French (woven) Ringlet Fronts*, and being so light and pretty, the ingenious way of making them, I think, ought to be preserved.

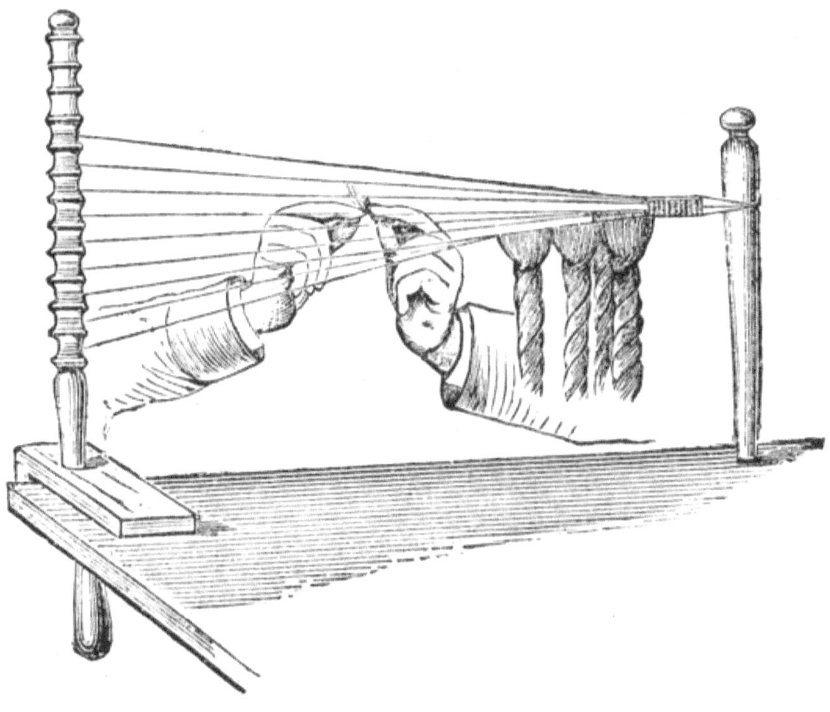

Fig. 21.

The weaving frame, then, resembles that which was before shown, but has more silks upon it. The peg is specially made for this kind of work, and there are a number of grooves for the silks, but one with twelve spaces will perhaps answer every purpose. Wind the silks upon it in the usual way, and tie up in groups of three according to the customary mode. Let each knot (which forms a stop to the weft) be in a line, thus—: and have nine of the silks placed in position as shown in the illustration.[12] Take first a piece of straight hair of the same colour as the curls, and about twelve inches long, and draw out what is best described as a coarse weft. This has to be plaited, as it were, upon all the silks employed in making the "front." Hold the root end between the thumb and finger of the left hand, having the long hair uppermost. Commence by placing it at the back of the lower silk, and draw it through. Then over two, under (or behind) three, over two and behind the top one. Continue in the same fashion downwards, but reversing the movement until the whole of the hair is worked up. Plait tight; but it can be made close and firm by pulling the hair as frequently as possible to get it into shape. (See the ends and centre of the next engraving.) Having thus worked the hair, finish off at the lower three silks by drawing the ends towards you, and leave it so for the present. Take three-quarters of an ounce, or an ounce of twelve-inch ringlet hair, and divide into two equal parts, bearing in mind that the curls have to be separated and classed together, and also that curls should always turn to the face, as I have

---

[12] Fig. 21.

repeatedly stated. Place the proper portion into the drawing brushes, and weave five inches of moderately fine close weft upon the three lower silks. Next make four inches and three-quarters of the same description of weft upon the three middle silks, leaving a quarter of an inch space between the end of the plait and the weft; the reason for doing so will presently appear. Now weave five inches of the same kind of weft upon the three top silks, and the end of each row must be regular. Draw off another coarse strand of the straight hair, and plait all the silks together as before. Three rows of weft are now to be done exactly the same, leaving the quarter of an inch space at the corresponding end; then take a third strand of straight hair and make a finishing plait as at the beginning. The whole length of the "front" should be eleven inches, including the plaited ends, and centre piece. The above illustration is so plain that no mistake can possibly arise if proper attention be given to the subject. Comb out the hair as each row is completed, and form into curls. Now warm a pair of pinching irons, press each section of the weft, and carefully remove with the scissors all superfluous ends and hairs. Cut the centre silk of each group of three, finish off securely and then cut down. I said just now that the reason for leaving the space at the ends of the middle row of weft would shortly appear, and you are now to take hold of those three silks and pull them. Do so at each end, the result will be to shorten the centre row; thus enabling you, with the help of springs, to form the mount as designed.[13] Make two springs, file down the ends, cover with kid or parchment, and sew them up in narrow galloon. Stitch the sides nicely, and fix them to each row of weft by means of a needle and silk. The springs may be about two inches long, and, of course, must be put on carefully. Strings of galloon are to be affixed, and so far as the making is concerned, the job is finished.

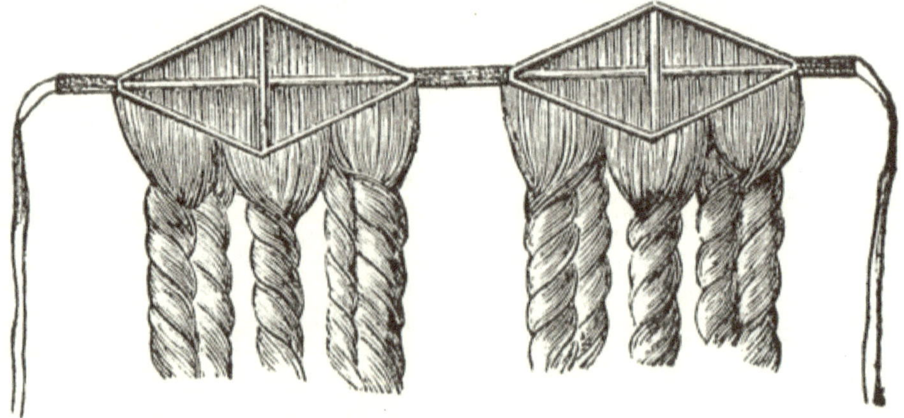

Fig. 22.

It is now to be placed upon a block, pressed and dressed as indicated in the wood-cut (p. 62). The number of curls is immaterial, for the hair may be arranged in three upon each side, or there might be as many as a dozen.

---

[13] Fig. 22.

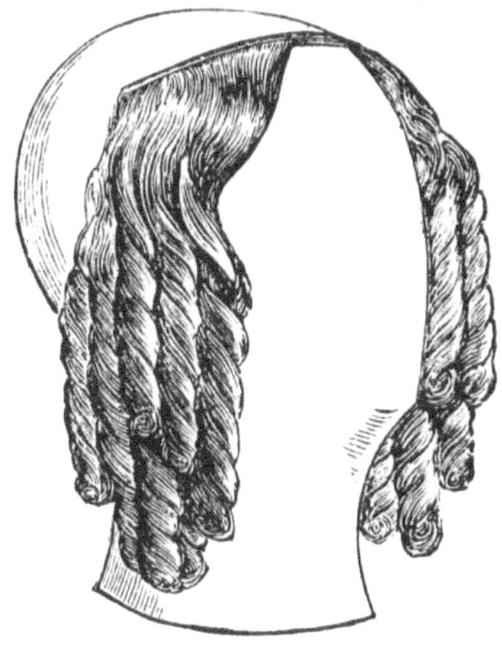

Fig. 23.

In addition to the kind just described, there is another way of proceeding so as to introduce a patent silk, or skin parting. These fronts can be made very light, and seeing that there is no net and but little galloon, ventilation does not suffer impediment. Proceed as follows:—Set up the weaving frame as shown in Fig. 21, but instead of nine silks there are now to be twelve. Tie them in threes as before, and intertwine a piece of straight, twelve-inch hair according to the following directions:—Hold the root end, pointing downwards, firmly between the thumb and finger of the left hand, and also the lower silk. Push the long hair through, pass two silks, and bring the hair to the front again. Then pass three, push the hair through, and pass three more, draw it forward, pass two, and over the top one. The hair plait (for plait it is) is now to be continued downwards, but the movements are to be reversed. I will describe this in another way. Say that you are holding the hair in the manner set forth above, together with the first lowest silk—now—over one, under two, over three, under three, over two, under one, and over the top, reversing the order of plaiting up and down till the length of hair is all used. You must "manœuvre" or work it a little, so as to get it tight, firm, and regular, and fasten off as previously instructed. Take three-quarters of an ounce, or an ounce, of ringlet hair of the required length, say ten or twelve inches. Separate the curls, putting all those which turn one way together, and do the same with the other lot. Bear in mind that curls should always turn to the face. Weigh the two portions, so that you may have an equal quantity of hair to work with. Make four inches and three-quarters of weft on the lower silks; four-and-a-half inches of weft on the next group; a like quantity on the group above, and five-and-a-quarter inches of weft upon the top. There is to be a vacancy of a quarter of an inch (near the plait) in the second and third rows, and this will explain why they differ from the lower one. As there is to be a patent parting, a space of an inch and a-half (but this depends upon the width of the parting) must be left in the centre to which you have now arrived; the top row forming an exception, and that is to be woven right along, without any break whatever.

Commence weaving in the order just described upon the other side, leaving the quarter-inch spaces at the ends of the second and third rows as before. Complete the weaving of the top row; see that the weft joins properly in the middle, because all should be uniform and regular. Make a corresponding plait to that which you did at the beginning; pinch the weft with warm irons; fasten off securely, and cut down.

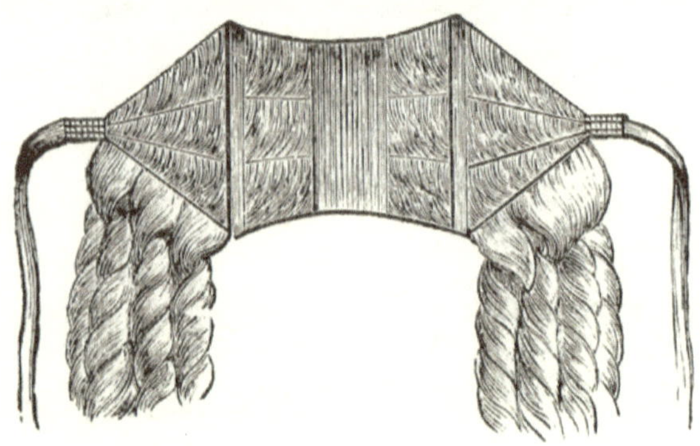

Fig. 24.

It has now to be mounted. Take a clean wig-block—there are two kinds, let me observe, "mounting" blocks and "combing" blocks—but it is to the former that I am alluding. Partings vary in depth, but the front here pourtrayed is four inches deep, and I will assume that you are going to make a similar one. Have some ribbon the full width of the parting (after the edges of the latter are tacked), and cut off five inches. Turn up the lower edge of the ribbon and lay the smooth surface upon the block, exactly in the centre, and just where the front should be worn when upon the head. Drive two points into the block, at short but equal distances from each other; take a needle and cotton, single, tie a knot, and "fasten on" to a point: pass the needle through one corner of the ribbon, and secure the cotton to the point below. Proceed in the same way with the other corner. Turn the block round, bend up the end of the ribbon as before, and secure the corners by means of basting stitches in a like manner. Remember, that in weaving I directed quarter-inch spaces to be left at both ends of the two inner rows of weft. Now draw the silks out a quarter of an inch so as to bring the weft close to the plait, for by this movement you will be enabled to spread out the top and bottom rows to the ends of the springs, while the centre rows are tightened and nearly straight, as they should be. Next sew the strings on to the plaited ends; make two springs, each a full quarter of an inch deeper than the parting; cover as previously instructed, and fix in their appointed places. (Fig. 24 clearly pourtrays all that is here described.) The two middle rows of weft need not be sewn to them yet. Now place all upon the block, get the mounted ribbon exactly in the middle, take hold of the strings, pull tight and drive a point through them at the back, in the place where they should be tied by the wearer. Arrange so as to keep the top row of hair out of the way; let the lower silks be a quarter of an inch above the place where the parting touches the forehead, and fix all in their respective positions by means of a needle and silk. Secure the two middle rows of weft to the springs in the same way. Now to affix the parting. Turn in the edges of the silk or skin upon which the parting is worked, and "tack" them in such a manner that the lowest portion (being the most important) is turned up last. The parting is now to be sewn neatly to the ribbon, commencing at the bottom; both should exactly fit, and, what is most important, only the parting is to be seen where it touches the brow.

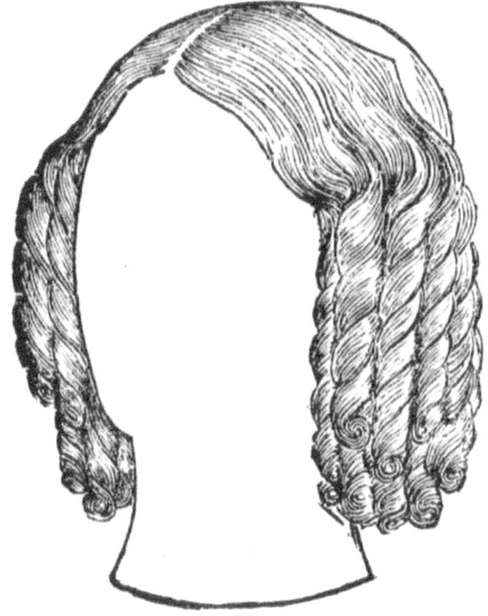

Fig. 25.

The pressing iron can now be used, the curls—be they many or few—arranged, a pair of side-combs placed in position if desired, and the front is finished, as above shown.

There are other fronts with ringlet curls beside those just described. For instance, there is a mounted front of a diamond shape, which is made to slide, technically called a *"diamond"* front. It is made as follows: cut off two pieces of galloon about eight or nine inches in length each. Sew the ends (through and through, not over and over) neat and firm; these are for the two sides. Place one of them upon a block, in the position it is intended to be worn. The ends of the galloon (where it has been sewn) must be uppermost at any place except a corner. Open the ends and hammer slightly, so as to make them lie as flat as possible. Take four points, and spread out the galloon in a diamond shape, so that it will be about two inches deep, and perhaps four inches long. Now take your needle and cotton, points, &c., and baste out in the required form; the upper and lower bastings (where the springs go) to be somewhat pointed; the ends are to be square, equal to the width of the galloon forming the strings. Make another mounting on the corresponding side of the block, and both must be alike in every particular. Upon the block (between the right and left sides of the mountings) a space of two inches or more should be left, because the wearer's own hair must be seen when the curls are worn. Bear in mind this is to be a sliding front, and the lady will be able to adjust the curls to her own wishes or taste. Now, the two sides being in their proper positions, and firmly secured by means of the basting stitches, sew a piece of galloon *on one side only* from one end to the other; the reason for doing so will presently be given. Cut off sufficient galloon for the strings, and this must be long enough to encircle the head, leaving plenty to tie in a double bow as well. Find the centre of the galloon, and temporarily fasten it with a point between the mounts. One of these strings is to be continued along the mount, corresponding with that upon which a piece of galloon has been sewn, the remainder being fastened by means of a point in the neck. The other half is to be abruptly turned back over the crown, and temporarily secured to keep it out of the way. Measure off two springs, grind the ends, cover with narrow galloon as previously instructed, and fix in their respective places. Put on the net; sew it to the inner edges of the mount only, and to both sides of the centre galloons and springs. The mountings are now ready for the hair.

Take sufficient hair, say one ounce of twelve-inch ringlet, and divide it equally. Weave a top row first, and ordinary front weft with the remainder. Do the same with the second lot of hair. Remember what I have said before—"All curls should turn to the face." Sew on the weft, beginning at the bottom of the lower galloon, turn the corners neatly; let the weft appear in regular rows, and, lastly, sew on the top row. Comb out the hair and curl it over the fingers in proper form before doing the other side, which, when done, is to be treated in a similar manner. Warm your pressing iron, divide the weft in conveniently small portions, and press carefully. Take the mountings off the block, and now I will give my reason for sewing on the first piece of galloon, namely, because this is the mounting intended to slide. Cut off another piece of galloon an inch longer than appears to be necessary. Turn in about half an inch at one end, and sew the corners securely to one of the ends of the mount. Neatly stitch the edge of this piece of galloon to the edge of that which is attached to the mount, but before fastening off, turn in the free end as you did at the beginning. Sew along the other edge of the galloon as before, and secure the stitches. Now there is a hollow space for the string to travel through, and a bodkin is the necessary instrument for leading it in the first instance. Replace the front upon the block, dress and arrange the curls as required.

Wing Fronts are made in a similar way, but instead of being of a diamond form they are shaped like birds' wings; the narrow end, of course, towards the upper part of the head, and the broad part near the ears. Mounts of this shape are very pretty, the curls lie nicely together, and, furthermore, they are easy to wear.

Bandeaux, or as they are more generally termed, "bands," embrace a variety of designs to suit different requirements. Some are made plain with a patent parting of silk or skin; others have net, gauze, or human hair foundations, and latterly a material called "Yak-hair" has been used, which answers the same purpose, and is less expensive. Then, again, there are *bandeaux* with waved hair or waved hair and "fringes," while others have long hair attached for combing in with the natural hair at the back. Indeed, this branch of the business offers a wide field for the display of taste, judgment, and ability. The hair used to be "banded" and then secured at or near the end of the mount, and dressing "bands" and "fronts" in the days of my apprenticeship was a continual source of employment and profit. The hair, at the time I speak of, was generally worn smooth, oils and pomades were in request, and rough hairdressing, it was thought, showed want of skill on the part of the hairdresser. But styles are ever-changing, and what is approved to-day will, perhaps, be condemned to-morrow. From smooth hairdressing we come to that which is dry, wavy, frizzy and crisp, and I am disposed to think that ladies sometimes imagine a coiffure should present a rough appearance to obtain approval. This loose method of arranging the hair is to the advantage of *bandeaux*, and coverings for bald places, because the false piece can be more easily arranged by the wearer.

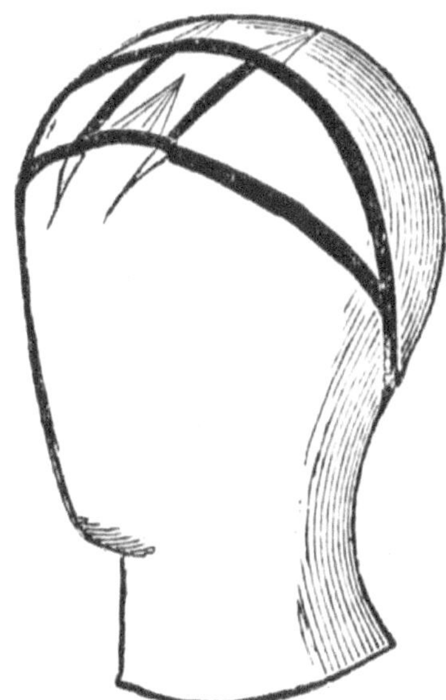

Fig. 26.

To make a plain bandeau, take a yard and a-half of galloon, measure ten inches from one of the ends but do not cut it off. Turn it back and give it two or three raps with the hammer so as to make a mark. Keep the galloon even and smooth, and turn back another ten inches at the other end; both of which are to be brought together. The ends are to be turned in, and stitched over and over. Double these sewn pieces exactly in the centre, and tap with the hammer again. Open out, and you will find that a mount of between nine and ten inches is begun. Now take a mounting block, which should be clean and smooth, and place the galloon thereon. The centre of the mount has already been found, and after opening it (say) two inches, temporarily fix by means of points in the centre of the block. There is no difficulty about this because a fine line marks the place, and I need scarcely say the mount should be on the block exactly as it is intended to be worn on the head. With the block in your lap (the face being turned inwards) take the galloon in each hand, pull tight, double one piece over the other, and drive a point through both at the back of the neck. Hammer it down firmly, and then fix the remainder of the galloon, which I need hardly say is intended for the strings, as you think proper, so long as they are out of your way. I will now suppose that you are going to make a three-inch silk or skin patent parting band, therefore you must commence with basting the lower galloon first, and then the top one, drawing it back at the same time, so as to give the necessary depth. Indeed, if you make it a rule to give a quarter of an inch more depth than the parting, it will be, I think, all the better. Next draw back the lower centre, and form a pretty curve, the object being to keep the galloon out of the way lest it be seen in the most critical part of your work, and, further, that the parting should lie upon the forehead both flat and close. Having done basting, the next thing is to put on the springs. Break two pieces of watch spring the proper length; the ends of which are to be rounded off and covered with kid or parchment, afterwards neatly enclosing the springs in galloon. They should have just sufficient bend to easily fit the head, and assist in holding the parting in position. A reference to the engraving will illustrate all that I have endeavoured to explain.[14]

Having well secured the mount which, let me say, should always be tight and firm upon the block, take a piece of ribbon, exactly the width of the centre between the springs, and sew thereon, the object of this being to give a neat appearance to the band when off the block, and, also, to conceal the work in the parting which otherwise could be seen. The net should next be attached, as directed in previous instructions, and then the mount will be completed.

In addition to the parting, take an ounce of the best hair (say) sixteen inches long (the hair in the parting being of the same length), and weave a top row. Weave the remainder of the hair in rather fine front weft, and then divide, marking the division, however, by merely tying a piece of string in the place. The parting should next be dealt with; turn in the edges as previously directed, "tacking" as you proceed, and finishing with the lower portion. Sew the parting in its proper position, beginning with the two corners in front; it will then be as well to sew it at the top, and afterwards the sides. The parting should be straight, and exactly in the centre; perfectly smooth, and not stretched or puckered in any direction. The weft must be sewn on next, but should there be a rather wide space between the parting and the top edge of the galloon, put in two or three rows of weft first. Sew the weft along the bottom and top edge of the galloon and then at regular intervals until one side is completed. Do the same with the other side, and, finally, put on

---

[14] Fig. 26.

the top row.

The number of rows will, of course, depend upon the quantity of weft, of which you must be the judge, and calculate accordingly. Press, tie the hair of each side together or loosely plait in three, leaving the wearer to arrange it when upon the head.

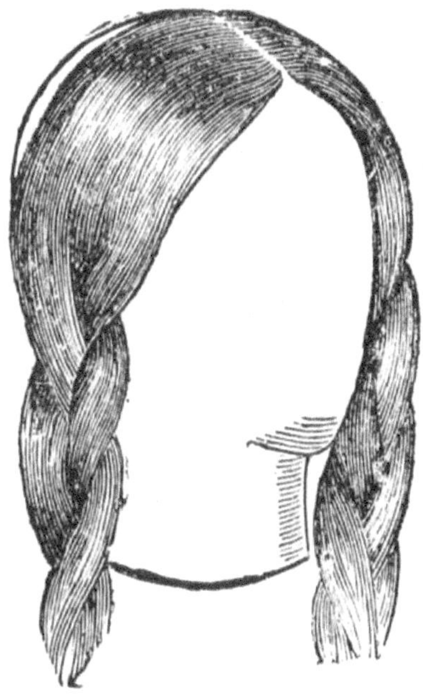

Fig. 27.

What I have already said is sufficient to show the learner how to make a "band" with a parting of either silk or skin, or any other similar substance. Indeed, when a "band" has to be produced for a very low price, it can be made without a patent parting at all, as the parting can be made to consist of weft only. To do this, the springs need not be so wide apart, and the intervening space is to be filled up with weft, sewn close, one row after the other, beginning at the bottom. If the weft is well done and fine, it will lie flat, then, with the comb, a parting should be made, and pressed into shape. True, the wearer cannot show the parting, but such work is designed for elderly ladies, and the cap border, or other head-gear hides it completely. Partings are generally used, however, and I merely allude to this very plain way of making a "band" to suit humble and, necessarily, economical customers.

For making a *Waved Bandeau, with fringe,* turn to the instructions for mounting already given, and notice the mount upon the block. A mount of a similar description is to be made, but *without* the arched piece of galloon in the centre, for the parting being of a transparent material, the skin of the head should be seen through it. Besides, a dark line of galloon just in the most conspicuous spot would be sadly out of order.

Proceed as follows: Take a clean block, and mark with a pencil the exact dimensions of the mount, in its proper place. Be very particular about this, because the pencilled lines you should strictly adhere to. These lines, then, having been made, commence by driving a point through the end of the galloon near the crown, and on your right side as the tracing faces you. Continue the galloon down to the angle upon the forehead where the spring goes, and fix with a point. Keep the galloon flat, and turn it towards the ear where it is also to be secured. Pass the galloon along the top, and when in the centre of the block (being mindful of the depth of the parting) drive in another point. For the other side continue the galloon as before, and end on the top of the block in a corresponding position to that where it begins. The mount should then resemble the illustration to which your attention is directed (Fig. 26), but with this difference—the centre arched portion of the galloon is absent.

The galloon is now to be "basted," and preceding instructions observed. The mount being tight and firm, the strings are to be neatly sewn on, fixed in the neck, and the long ends put out of the way as before. It is now seen that there is a gap in the centre, and unless some kind of stay is put at the lower part, the parting will, in all probability, soon get torn. To obviate this, it is usual to employ a material called "silk-worm gut," which is securely fastened across the bottom, or nearly at the bottom, for the parting should be so arranged as to lie flat on the forehead—the closer it lies the better. Sometimes a white horse hair is used for the purpose, and occasionally white silk, but whatever the material, it should be strong and durable. It is usual, also, to put additional "stays" about an inch apart, right along the parting, for they are not seen upon the head, and much greater strength is given to the article. Indeed, when the parting is more than three inches deep it is absolutely necessary to do so.

Put on the springs as before, let them be narrow, and in this instance they may be covered with black tape, as the galloon upon which they will be sewn conceals them from view when off the block. Now attach the net, and the mounting is completed.

A mount, let me observe, should be accurately designed, and measurements taken from any convenient place upon the block must correspond, one side with the other. Indeed, where much board-work is done, it is a strong recommendation to be a good "mounter," and a correct eye is not among the least of such a man's qualifications. It matters not how well done the knotting, weaving, or sewing may be; should the mount be inexact, the work is faulty from the very commencement, and might result in the article being returned. This is best avoided. Therefore, make it a rule to "start fair" with your work, and, if slow, be sure, remembering at all times that "practice makes perfect," and how important it is that strict attention should be paid to minute details.

The mount having been finished, the next thing is to put in a transparent parting, with a "fringe." This "fringe" should be of short, curled hair, which can be arranged when the job is finished. In transparent partings generally there are no edges to turn up, like those made of silk or skin, and alluded to before. Commence by sewing the parting to the corner of the mount on your right hand first, finish off, and then attach it to the corresponding corner on the left side, keeping the line of parting exactly in the middle. It will then be proper to sew the top; see that it is firm, straight, and smooth, and conclude by stitching the sides. About the same length and quantity of hair will be required for this as was used in the previous one; therefore, weave a top row, divide the weft, and proceed according to the instructions already given. Sew the weft on in rows, beginning at the bottom; neatly and securely turn the corners; and, lastly, affix the top row. Press, and dress as required; take it off the block, draw out the basting stitches, and the work is done, unless you wish to give a waviness to the hair.

Fig. 28.

Of course the hair can be left straight if desired, but if waved (it need not be very strong), the effect is much more natural. Put the band on the block again, and the hair can be waved in either of the following ways:—(1) *By plaiting.* Slightly damp the hair, and make two or more three-plaits upon each side. Plait rather tight, and pinch with moderately warm irons, but only sufficient to remove the moisture, if any, and to fix the wave. This, perhaps, is the most simple and natural way of doing it. (2) *With hair-pins.* Divide the side-hair in two or three equal portions, so as to make the wave regular and uniform. Take a long hair-pin, and with the left hand hold it close to the roots of one of the pieces, keeping the prongs rather wide apart. Then, with the right hand, entwine the piece of hair in and out, as though forming with it any number of figures 8. Having come to the ends (or done as much as you consider necessary), push up close to the head of the pin, turning back one of the points to keep the hair well in place. Do the same with all; pinch with warm irons, and allow it to be quite cold before drawing out the pins. (3) Curling-irons are used also for waving the hair, but, although permissible when dressing a lady's hair, I do not advise their use for work of this description. There are other methods of waving hair, as with string, card, wire, etc., but what I have described, if carefully done, will answer nearly all requirements.

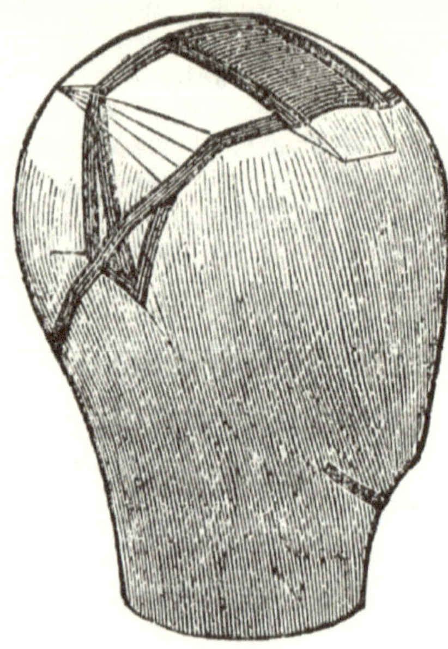

Fig. 29.

Temple-Mounted Fronts.—Measure off twenty-three inches of galloon, double it, and stitch at the ends through and through. Shift the ends a little, so that they will come anywhere but where basting stitches are likely to be put. Now double the galloon again, tap it with the hammer, open it, and you will find that you have made two creases. Put these creases upon the line which marks the centre of the block, and fix them with points to about the depth of the parting. Take other points and bring the mount into shape. You will now require a rule, or tape measure, a pair of compasses, and a large double-threaded needle, to enable you to make correct measurements. You can measure from any convenient spot, but when the strings are on, they should be so adjusted that, when off the block and tightened, the mount will incline inwards both at top and bottom, thus proving that it will bind, or fit well to the head. The shape is well defined in the illustration,[15] and the places where basting stitches are to be put distinctly shown. Springs are made and fixed on the top about the width of the parting, the intervening space being filled up with a piece of ribbon. A spring is also placed on each side near the ear, so as to keep the mount well in shape, and the strings, as will be seen, are made to cross over from the bottom galloon to the top. The trained eye will perceive at a glance how comfortable this shaped mount is likely to be to the wearer.

Having sewn on the net, commencing, as usual, upon the inner edge of the lower galloon, the next thing is to put in the parting, which should be either skin or silk—but if transparent a deviation will have to be made as already explained. The same remark applies as to whether the hair should be knotted or woven. These matters must always be decided upon at first, when the mount is commenced.

---

[15] Fig. 29.

Take (say) 1¼ oz. of twelve-inch ringlet hair, and put the curls in two lots as usual. Weigh one parcel against the other, and balance evenly. Remember what I have said about the curls inclining to the face. Make a thin top row, comb out, and cut down. Weave the hair in fine front weft, and contrive to make it of a similar length for both sides. Commence sewing on at or near the string, and proceed as before instructed. In stitching on the weft be careful to well secure the net, and the spaces must be according to the length of the weft used—certainly they should not be so much as a quarter of an inch apart. Let both sides be uniform and alike in every respect. Press and dress as required, and retain the hair in position by means of side-combs. If, at the outset, it is decided to "knot" the hair, then the mount should be prepared accordingly, respecting which I have given instructions in another place.[16]

Fillets (or Cauls).—A fillet signifies a little band intended to tie about the hair; and a caul (probably a modification of *cowl*) intimates, in trade parlance, a net or some such covering for the head. But that which I am going to describe is probably unknown to many, although it was formerly adopted by elderly women instead of a wig. This can be accounted for in two or three ways. (1) Because at the time I speak of "fronts" were generally worn; (2) ladies' wigs were heavy and expensive, and (3) a fillet or caul, being much cheaper, well answered the purpose. Indeed, where the necessity exists for wearing a head covering, through loss of hair, or other causes, perhaps a fillet would be most acceptable to many in want of some such assistance. Proceed as follows: Measure the head, and use a mounting-block about one inch larger in size. Put on any shaped mount you please so long as it is adapted to the purpose, and suits the requirement of the lady for whom it is in-tended. In place of strings use a piece of wide galloon which is neatly attached to the mount, and fits comfortably round the head. The galloon may be half an inch or more in width, or a mount can be made in the neck (extending from ear to ear) resembling that portion of a lady's wig. Having the mount, springs, and wide gal-loon in position, you have next to obtain a silk net, and put it on to the block, cover-ing the entire mount and neck-piece as well.[17] The meshes of the net should not be too open, because the weft has to be sewn upon a part of it. I need hardly observe that no portion of the net must be allowed to project over the lower edges of the galloon and mount. The hair is now to be divided as before; a top-row woven, and good front, or "twice-in" weft made. Bear in mind that instead of sewing it along the lower galloon, and turning at the parting and strings, it is now to be sewn from bottom to top; in other words—begin sewing on the weft where the wide galloon joins; let the hair incline or fall over the ear, and, as I said just now, sew the weft from bottom to top, turning each row upon the lower and upper galloon. The rea-son is, that as the meshes are much more open than in the ordinary description of net, the rows of weft ought to be shortened so as to give additional strength. Hav-

[16] Page 78.

[17] There are (or used to be) silk nets made for the purpose, very strong and durable, and could be procured where the "trimmings" are usually sold. The crown of this net is left rather loose and threaded on a silk cord. The cord is held up, which gathers the loose meshes together, when it should all be fastened, and thus a caul net well fitting the head is formed.

ing finished the front part, attention must now be directed to the back, or rather that portion which fits in the neck and extends from ear to ear. Have ready (say) half an ounce of "Sevigny," or "doll" hair. This is tight curled hair of about four or five inches in length—the same in fact as that used in making "fringes." Weave very fine, and sew on to the wide galloon, turning at each end of it. The long and short hair will thus meet near the front of the ear, where the joining must be neat.

If the hair is to be worn either plain or wavy and banded, of course hair (say) of sixteen inches in length should be used, but if in curls, probably ten or twelve-inch hair will be sufficient. Dress as required. The short-curled hair (after the work is pressed) can be arranged in small ring curls, or in the manner of a close fringe.

Remember, I said that a block somewhat larger than the head was to be used, and the reason is plain. The fillet is sure to be large enough, and this will allow for shrinking; besides, there is to be an elastic spring put in the neck which must be done so as to grip or bind the head properly. If these details are carefully attended to, the fillet will fit "like a glove," be a source of comfort to the wearer, and a credit to the maker. How an elastic spring is to be placed and held in position will appear in due course.

CHAPTER IX.

General Observations on the Manufacture of Partings and Crowns—
Non-transparent Partings; Silk and Skin—Transparent Partings;
Net, Gauze, Yak, and Human Hair Foundations—"The Genealogy of Implantation"—Knotting, and some remarks thereon—Single Knotting—Double Knotting.

Partings, no matter for what use they may be intended, are either transparent
or opaque. The foundation of transparent partings is invariably net, gauze,
yak hair, or human (white) hair, the two latter substances being specially adapted
to the purpose. Indeed, anything that will enable the worker to imitate nature so
closely as to defy detection, might be employed, if it be durable and impervious
to the effects of perspiration—two points never to be overlooked. The great art of
parting-making is to cause the joining (where it comes in contact with the forehead) to be so exquisitely well done, that it passes unnoticed even by a keen-sight-
ed and critical observer. Now is a chance for some ingenious young man to make
himself famous, as perfection is not yet reached, I venture to think in this respect.
True, the "fringe" goes far to produce a natural appearance in those who are still
young, but a "fringe" is out of place altogether upon the brow of a matronly dame,
or attached to the parting of a gentleman's wig; therefore I repeat there yet remains
something to be done in the matter of partings, and probably a fortune awaits the
lucky inventor. But there are professed patent parting makers, and, as a rule, it is
most advisable to purchase this portion of the work ready made, or have it done
to order. When convenient, especially if a hairdresser resides at a distance from
London or certain provincial towns, it is expedient to keep a small stock of such
goods in the house, for occasionally it happens that an order is wanted in a hurry.
Most in request are partings of three, three and a-half and four inches deep, made
with hair sixteen or eighteen inches long, and, I may add, common colours. Here
then is a little "stock-in-trade" which is sure to come in useful. Should the reader,
however, wish to make the parting himself, I will merely say that "foundations" of
the usual length and width can be obtained through the usual trade channels, but
I may hazard an opinion, which is, that very few hairdressers execute this kind of
work themselves.

Non-transparent partings are made upon silk or skin, the latter consisting of a
very thin skin upon white or pale-pink silk. I have known other substances used
(more by way of an experiment than anything else) but the foundations named
are, so far as I am aware, universally employed. Silk partings are the cheapest, skin
partings and net partings come next, and so on, the price per inch being regulated

according to width, foundation, length and quality of the hair, workmanship, &c.

It is worthy of observation that fronts, in years gone by, were almost universally worn by married women. "The first grey hair" gave the signal, and a visit to the hairdresser followed shortly after. His aid was invoked, and, if holding a good position in the trade, his design was to produce a front natural in appearance, and sufficiently open in the parting, to suit the expression of the features. But since the introduction of silk and skin partings (which occasionally show a division little more than a straight line) the aim seems to be different, and a parting is produced thicker and closer than would be seen on a young girl's head. The result of this is to impart a heavy aspect to the countenance, which is at all times undesirable, and will account in some degree for their discontinuance. These unnatural-looking partings are sometimes demanded by persons who make no pretension to good taste, and they will not be advised by the tradesman, who knows full well what is likely to suit them best. Partings which require the most skill in their manufacture, if the aim be to produce a good article, are silk and skin partings, and to make the first of these proceed as follows:—In proportion to the length of parting required prepare a stout wire frame—say six inches long, and four inches wide, and that you are going to work a three and a-half inch parting. With the help of a needle and stout cotton, stretch the silk firm and secure in the centre of the frame, so that it is immovable and longer than required. Weave the hair in "close," or "once in" weft, keeping it free from grease or dirt lest the foundation be soiled. Attach the weft to the back of the silk, and draw a few hairs through at a time by means of a small hook made for the purpose. Work regularly and methodically, bearing in mind the width and length required. The centre portion must be done very fine, while the sides may be coarser, a somewhat larger hook being used. Having drawn all the hair through to what is now the top, take a comb and "make a parting" the same as you would upon a lady's head. Comb the hair smoothly on each side, warm the pressing-iron, and press into shape. Cut down, and the parting is made.

It is not reasonable to expect first attempts to afford much satisfaction, but procure a well-made parting and strive to imitate it by all the means in your power. With a good pattern, you may observe what *can* be done, and if you desire to enter the foremost ranks, you *must* endeavour to equal, if not excel others.

Skin partings are made the same way, but, as I have before said, a thin skin (sold for the purpose) is laid upon the silk before working.

Transparent partings are to be made upon a net, gauze, Yak-hair, or human-hair foundation. Professed patent-parting makers no doubt use a frame, but a hairdresser would, in all probability, make the parting upon a block, and in its proper place. Of course, it is best to do the parting as a separate portion, because it can be easier pressed into shape, and the piece of thin skin (previously sewn underneath) for preventing the effects of perspiration, will escape being punctured by the knotting needle. However, this is a matter for consideration by the worker, who must necessarily be somewhat experienced before venturing to knot partings. The kind of net used for partings can be purchased at a hair merchant's; it is made of cotton, and should be fine, smooth, and as regular as possible consistent with durability. Gauze is much finer and closer than net, being manufactured expressly for the purpose. It is largely used for scalpettes, gentlemen's scalps, and fine knotted work generally. *TulleYak*, or Yak-hair foundations, are made abroad, and well suit the purpose for which they are intended.

Like other work of this description, the meshes vary in size, and can be had either open or very close. But the best foundations are made of white human hair, with a square, round, diamond, or diamond-barred mesh; the foundations for crowns, and crowns and partings, being specially prepared. Speaking of the Yak-hair manufacture, a recent writer says, "there is a large quantity of good lace made in the mountain villages of Saxony and Bohemia, and thousands of hands are thus constantly employed. This industry has of late received an addition in the manufacture of a peculiar lace or *tulle* made of white hair. It was introduced into this district a few years ago by a Normandy lady, and has since then extended to such a degree that now in one town (Rothenkerchen) alone several hundred persons live by it. The lace is made of white human hair procured from all countries of Europe, but principally from Italy. The price paid for it ranges from one penny to two shillings per *gramme*, according to quality, and the fine lace made out of it is used as a foundation for wigs."

To give completeness to my work, a short account of "The Genealogy of Implantations," from the *Moniteur de la Coiffure*, will, no doubt, interest the reader, for it has a direct bearing on the subject.

The journal named had the following under the heading of "Croisat and the 101 Coiffeurs."

"In 1805, Leguet, hairdresser at Lyons, invented the flesh-coloured hair-net. *Postiches* had hitherto been so coarsely made that this improvement in the manufacture of wigs caused quite a sensation. The fame of the inventor soon reached Paris, and M. Tellier, hairdresser at the Palais Royal, tried to buy Leguet's patent. In 1810, Leguet, who had found that his wigs did not keep the desired firmness (the hair being badly knotted), easily agreed to cede his patent to Tellier. An English firm having heard of Leguet's invention, procured one of his wigs, which they imitated and improved. This came to the knowledge of Tellier, who went to London to study the improvements. Meanwhile, Carron, another coiffeur at the Palais Royal, bought from a Lyons silk weaver the process for the implantation on silk of a different kind, which, though less suitable for men's wigs than that of Leguet's, gave much neater partings for women's work. Tellier, on his return to Paris, intending to considerably extend his novel industry, associated himself with a stocking-weaver of the Cevennes. Hence arose a law suit between Carron and Tellier. But, contrary to the ordinary rule, this law suit, instead of ruining the parties more immediately concerned, helped to make their fortune. All the papers were full of this suit, and every baldhead—feminine or masculine—in the kingdom was eager to see and perchance try to rejuvenate itself by the novel inventions. The poor Lyons weaver, who had parted with his patent, being unable to witness others amassing fortunes by its means, while he remained in misery, put an end to his days. In the law suit M. Tellier, having produced the patent bought of Leguet, got the best of it.

"Michalon, a weaver, invented the silk parting, produced with a long piece of silk without head, which he put on his shuttle. Dufaur invented the knotted hair foundation, knotting the hair by means of a gauze needle. Then a workman established himself in the Faubourg St. Denis, who made partings in the way Carron made them. He was the first to make partings in heart shape. The brothers Lavacquerie perfected the work of the latter. Valon, one of Dufaur's workmen, further perfected the wigs by giving a tighter and better fit.

"In 1822, Souchard took out a patent at Bordeaux for implantations made with an embroidery needle, and having in the course of time perfected his invention, he tried to implant hair on a pig's bladder, which, being lined with *gros de Naples*, made an excellent bald-wig for theatrical performances, and produced a very good effect.

"In 1823 Souchard went to England, to study the manner in which the English made their silk net wigs. He found the English silk net infinitely superior to the French, and be adopted the former for his wigs.

"This genealogy of M. Souchard's was written in 1836, and since then implantation has made immense progress."

Enough, perhaps, has been said about the manufacture of partings to acquaint the reader with the manner in which this kind of work is done; but I regard parting-making as a separate branch, and only those who have constant practice can expect to become proficient.

Knotting, however, lies more within the hairdresser's domain, and to be a clever knotter the worker must be patient, careful, have good eyesight, and bring to bear sound judgment in the arrangement and execution of his work. In parts not seen, or rather where knots are concealed through being covered with the hair above, they may be somewhat coarsely done, but in conspicuous places, such as partings or crowns, the greatest skill must be exhibited, and Nature copied as exactly as possible. I have had occasion to refer at different times to knotting, and it will be well, perhaps, to speak of it in general terms before dwelling upon any class of work in particular.

In preparing a mount for knotting (no matter whether it be for a *bandeau*, front, scalp, scalpette, or what not) you have to decide first whether there is to be weft upon the edges of the net, and likewise upon the galloon. If so, the net need only be cut off as before mentioned; but when the mount is to be knotted all over, the edges of the net must be allowed to extend the eighth of an inch or more beyond the whole of the galloon. Here is the reason: in order to knot over the galloon and close to the edges of it, that portion of the net which projects must be turned under and in upon the galloon, to which it should be neatly and securely sewn. Indeed, the net must be sewn to the galloon wherever edges occur, for it not only holds the net firm and tight, but when taken off the block there are no ugly openings visible. Bear in mind the net is to be put on firm and tight, the meshes well open, and no "bagginess" in any part. There are different kinds of net, and you will have to select particular sorts for special work, about which experience—if no other instructor can be approached—must be your guide.

Fig. 30.

Knotting needles are, as the accompanying illustration shows, small hooks set in wooden handles, and can be purchased where the trimmings for wig-making, etc., are procurable. These needles are fine, medium, and coarse, each one being employed according to the kind of work required to be done. For instance, in knotting over galloon or ribbon, where the knots cannot be seen when the mount is examined, they might be coarsely done, especially if thickness of hair be required. Upon net, perhaps the medium-sized needle had better be used, but a needle sufficiently fine to carry only a single hair will have to be employed in partings and crowns if you attempt to "defy detection." Care is necessary in the selection of a needle, the point of which should turn, as it were, into the neck of it, otherwise, in drawing back, the hook is likely to catch the net, and your handiwork stands a chance then of being spoiled before it is completed. Let me here give one word of advice. When you have obtained needles to your liking, take the greatest care of them, for if you are proud of good workmanship they might come to be regarded as "little treasures."

The first thing a learner should do is to make a "single knot," and I would recommend that a mount be put on the block, say similar to that here shown, merely for the sake of practising.

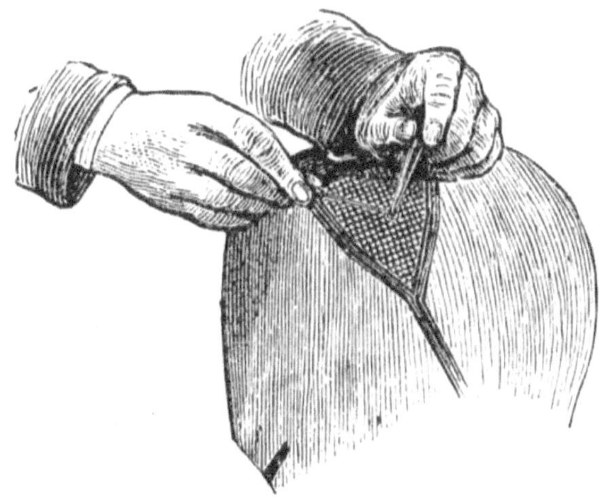

Fig. 31.

Take some straight hair about six inches long;[18] put it between the drawing brushes, and place a weight thereon as though you were going to do weaving.

[18] I mention six inches because hair of that length is most convenient for a learner to practise with, but you will have to knot hair of various lengths, from the shortest for gentlemen's *perukes,* to very long for ladies' wigs.

Draw out a weft and double it over at the roots, leaving them (the roots) rather long. You have now made a loop, which is to be held firmly between the thumb and finger of the left hand. Take the knotting needle and hold it with the thumb and finger of the right hand; insert the hook in one opening of the net and allow it to pass out at the next. By this movement you have taken up a thread (or line) upon which you are going to knot the hair. Now bring the looped portion of the hair forward and hook it with the needle; Fig. 31 clearly indicates the position. Turn the open part of the hook downwards, but keeping firm hold of the hair (by a little dexterity you may avoid catching hold of the net) and draw the needle back again. Let the open part of the hook now face the weft, and by a slight movement of the needle the loop will slip back a little towards the handle while you catch hold of or hook the weft again. This is well shown in the following illustration.

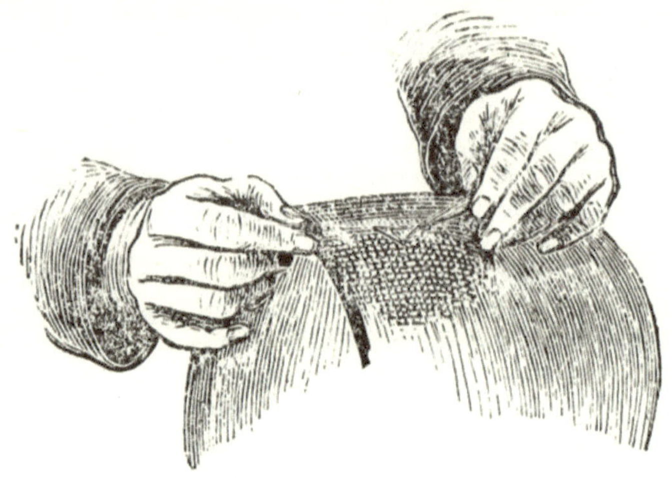

Fig. 32.

You have now to give it a turn (which to a certain extent secures the hair), draw the hook (with the hair) through the loop; let go the hair from the left hand at the same moment, and pull rather tight. The knot will then be upon the net, and if the roots are long fairly secure. Of course there is a difficulty in describing these technicalities, but I think with a little practice there need not be any trouble in mastering the details, at least so far as I have gone.

With regard to single knotting, I would observe that it is not so secure as double knotting, but the knots can and should be made much finer. In single knotting, the roots ought always to be long, much longer in fact than when the knots are double, and ought only to be done with a hair or two at a time, such very fine work being necessary in the middle of partings, the centres of crowns, etc. When single knots are coarsely made, they are liable to be caught by the comb when arranging the hair, and, as a consequence, the weft pulled out; but if finely worked this is not so liable to occur. Single knotting can be done rapidly with short hair, as in gentlemen's wigs, but it is somewhat insecure, and, therefore, best avoided. Better be "slow and sure" at your work, than spoil it altogether merely to be quick. Strive at all times to execute good work, so that your employer may depend upon what you do, and all that emanates from the shop will, in consequence, bear the stamp of excellence.

With regard to double knotting, I wish you to turn to the instructions given on page 79, and, to avoid recapitulation, begin with the words, "Take some straight hair," etc., and follow on till you come to "draw the hook (with the hair) through the loop," then stop for a moment and take up here. I repeat—"draw the hook (with the hair) through the loop;" let *that* slide back a little as it did before, take hold of (or hook) the weft again, giving the needle at the same moment a turn; draw through the loop once more, and pull tight down upon the net. In other words, proceed as though you were going to make a single knot, but instead of drawing it through at once, make another knot upon the hair itself, and then draw through. Thus you have made or tied a *double knot*, and there need not be any fear of its coming away, for it is too well secured. These double knots should be made where they are best concealed, but ought not to be coarsely done, otherwise they will appear unsightly when the workmanship is examined. Practice, with attention to details, will soon enable you to become expert. When the job is completed, (if it be a front, or a band, or anything of that description), have ready a top row of weft, and sew it on as before instructed, press, and finish off in the usual way.

CHAPTER X.

Of Wigs in General, and some Historical remarks thereon—On Taking
an Order for a Wig or Scalp—Means adopted for securing them
to the Head—Directions for Measurement—On Mounting and
Making a Scalp—"Pen-knife" and Metallic Springs—A Scalp described with Parting and Crown—Scalps with Gauze, Net, and
Human Hair Foundations.

Of wigs in general how much could be written! They are almost "as old as the hills," and perhaps amongst the ancient Egyptians might be found the earliest makers of the periwig, or peruke. Indeed, in the British Museum can be seen a wig from the Temple of Isis that was made two or three thousand years ago; the curl and material of which it is made being well preserved. Probably the custom of shaving the heads of the people (for all had to submit to it), led to the introduction of wigs, and, as Wilkinson says, "it may appear singular that so warm a covering to the head should have been adopted in the climate of Egypt; but we must remember the reticulated nature of the ground-work, on which the hair was fastened, allowed the heat of the head to escape, while the hair effectually protect-ed it from the sun: it is evident that no better covering could have been devised, and that it far surpassed, in comfort and coolness, the modern turban." According to Stow, the periwig was first brought into England about the time of the massacre of St. Bartholomew (1572), but the peruke is mentioned in a wardrobe account in the time of Edward VI. About 1595, wigs "had become so much the fashion that it was dangerous for children to wander out of sight of their parents or attendants, as it was a common practice to entice them into some private place and deprive them of their hair for the manufacture of such articles."—*Planche*. During the reign of Charles II. the large wigs (such as are shown in Kneller's portrait of the Duke of Marlborough) were introduced, and continued to increase in size till the middle of last century. Concerning prices, the following is interesting:—"Perukes," says Malcolm, "were an highly important article in 1734. Those of right gray human hair were four guineas each; light grizzle ties, three guineas; and other colours in proportion, to twenty-five shillings. Right gray human hair perukes, from two guineas to fifteen shillings each, which was the price for dark ones; and right gray bob perukes, two guineas and a-half to fifteen shillings, the price of dark bobs. Those mixed with horsehair were much lower. It will be observed, from the grada-tions in price, that real gray hair was most in fashion, and dark of no estimation."

The names of wigs, as may be judged from the foregoing, possess deep in-terest for the trade, and it is therefore worth while to allude to them. In the reign of Queen Anne, in addition to very long and formally curled perukes, are mentioned "black riding wigs," "bag wigs," and "nightcap wigs." The famous battle of Ramilies, in the same reign introduced the "Ramilie wig," with a long gradually diminishing plaited tail, called the "Ramilie tail," which was tied with a great bow at the top and a smaller one at the bottom. In the reign of George II., the "tye-wig" and the "pigtail-wig" have to be added to the catalogue, and at the same time the revival of the "bob-wig," first heard of in 1684, or one that is called after it, is also spoken of. The "bob-wig" is thus described:—"I cut off my hair and procured a brown bob periwig of Wilding of the same colour, with a single row of curls just round the bottom, which I wore very nicely combed and without powder." Indeed, "the nomenclature of wigs is very ample," says an authority on the subject, "a complete system of classification might be adopted, and genus and species discriminated with the greatest nicety: there were Wigs Military, Legal, Ecclesiastical, and Infantile," room being found only for a few varieties, viz.:—

Perruque à bonnet.	Perruque à la brigadière.
Perruque à nœuds.	Perruque de l'Abbé.
Perruque ronde.	Perruque à boudin.
Perruque pointue.	Perruque à papillons.
Perruque naissante.	Perruque à deux marteaux.
Perruque à deux queues.	Perruque à trois marteaux
Perruque à tonsure.	Perruque à bourse.

Wigs were first worn by barristers about 1670, to which opposition was made by the judges, and some of the leaders were not allowed to plead in their new head-gear. In the time of James II. wigs increased in size, becoming still larger in the following reign (William III.), when wigs were adopted by all classes, but among those of humble station they were moderate in size and price. Gentlemen's wigs, however, were large and full, requiring much hair in their manufacture. It is recorded that in 1700 a sum of £60 was given for a country girl's hair, and that the grey hair of an old woman deceased sold for nearly as much—the ordinary price of a first-class wig being at that time forty pounds. Full-bottomed wigs were invented, it is said, by Duviller, for the purpose of hiding some natural defect in the shoulders of the Dauphin. Children wore wigs, or the natural hair was curled to look like them. Archbishop Tillotson was the first of our prelates who wore a wig. Steele's wig cost as much as forty guineas. Dean Swift had a fine wig for state occasions, and "Colley Cibber's wig, in which he played a favourite character, was of such noble proportions that it was brought upon the stage in a sedan by two chairmen." The tie-wig (the long-curled wig abridged) was not considered court dress.

"How to wear a wig," says the author of "Trichocosmos," "was part of the education of a man of the world, not to be learned from books. Those who know what witchcraft there is in handling a fan, what dexterity in the 'nice conduct of a clouded cane,' will imagine the wits and gentlemen of old did not suffer the wig to overshadow their temples with perpetual gloom, like the wreath of smoke which overhangs our Modern Babylon. And many a country squire must have tried in vain to catch the right toss of the head; to sport a playful humour in those crisp curls; or to acquire the lofty carriage of the foretop, or the significant trifling with some obtrusive lock; and felt as awkward in his new wig as a tailor on horseback, or a fat alderman with a dress sword dangling between his legs."

Natural coloured wigs were worn till about 1714, when it became fashionable to adopt bleached hair, which soon faded, then wigs were powdered. It is said that wigs of peculiar excellence cost as much as £140 each, and it is on record that "a petition from the master peruke-makers of London and Westminster, presented to the king (George III.) in 1763, points out the great decline of their use to have taken place at that time." In this memorial they complain of the public wearing their own hair, and say, "That this mode, pernicious enough in itself to their trade, is rendered excessively more so, by swarms of French hairdressers already established in those cities, and daily increasing."

Theatrical wigs will supply many capital illustrations of those that were worn by notable personages in former years, and a ramble through the National Gallery, Hampton Court Palace, and other public as well as private picture galleries will be found highly instructive to wig-makers of the present day. The chief art now consists in making wigs so closely to imitate Nature as to defy detection, and those who succeed in doing so may well be classed among the most talented men in the profession. Wigs and scalps will always be worn, and probably there is a good trade to be done in such manufactures now, but great attention to every detail is necessary so as to withstand the keen glance of scrutiny.

I will now apply myself to the task before me, but consider that a few general observations are necessary and important before entering into the technicalities of the art.

When taking an order for a lady's or gentleman's wig, observe the shape of the head, cast of countenance, and age of the person who intends wearing it. Note whether the head is long, broad, or high, as a correct shape ought to be maintained by the wig-maker, who, in this and other respects, should be an artist. Observe also whether the face is long, round, or oval, because the arrangement of the hair on the forehead and sides of the head has much to do in presenting a good appearance. If this passes observation and comment, the result may be considered satisfactory; but should there be "a something" objectionable which causes remark, find out what it is, or where the fault lies, and either remove or alter it if possible. Again, notice the countenance; do not put in contrast to an aged face hair that is only suitable to youth. Let the hair be consistent both in colour and quantity with the age of the wearer, and, above all, endeavour to avoid anything extravagant or out of place. A gentleman's wig must be cut and trimmed after it is made, to adapt it to the style and taste of the wearer; it ought to fit easily in every part; and where springs are, no undue pressure should be allowed to exist. While the general appearance has to be well considered, the comfort of the wearer must always be kept in view.

The reader is, doubtless, fully aware that baldness is not confined to age, for some men lose their hair early in life. You may, without much trouble, find a bald-headed man at thirty, and it is perhaps as easy to discover a man at sixty with a fairly good head of hair. All classes are likely to be more or less troubled with baldness, for it makes its mark in a variety of ways. Sometimes the hair recedes from the brow, giving the appearance of a very high forehead, at other times it only attacks the crown. Then, again, the whole of the top part of the head is left bare, which not unfrequently extends to the occiput behind. A partial baldness requires merely a scalp which may, according to the circumstances of the case, be either large or small, but when the baldness is extensive, a wig will be found the most convenient and suitable head-covering. Scalps are consequently made in a variety of shapes and sizes; the mountings are equally variable, and the method adopted for holding them firmly in position admits of great ingenuity. Some scalps are mounted with galloon, net, and springs; others have a metallic-spring attachment, which sensibly, though not uncomfortably, grips the head, while another mode of fastening is by means of "penknife springs" or clasps.[19] (These open as the name indicates, and being closed, a small portion of the growing hair is shut in or clasped at the same time.) Some scalps, when made for the top of the head and crown have, in addition, a strip of galloon, which, being covered with hair, easily adapts itself to the lower part of the back of the head. By an arrangement of this character a scalp cannot possibly go forward on to the forehead of the wearer. Scalps when made very light and delicate, and intended for a small-sized patch upon the upper portion of the head, and sometimes the crown, are fixed only with gum, a gummy substance sold for the purpose, or diachylon. This gossamer-like scalp admits of very superior work (knotted), while the mounting, if required, should be of the lightest possible description. Where strength and durability are concerned, probably nothing can be better than a well-sewn, woven scalp or wig; but when art steps in to closely imitate nature, and attempts to defy the keen glance of scrutiny, then both single and double knotting are brought into requisition. This presents a more natural appearance, of course, and though the cost is increased, the work is not so lasting. In wig and scalp making there is plenty of scope for ability, ingenuity, and taste, for to insure success very much is left to the judgment of the maker, and to the carefulness and discretion of the wearer, so as to prevent his "secret" being discovered. I will give some working directions, with suitable illustrations, as I proceed, but for the present I am chiefly concerned in impressing certain leading points or features upon the mind of the learner, as success will greatly depend upon strict attention to minute details.

Of course, careful measurement is all important, for no matter how well the work may be done, if it proves to be a misfit, disappointment and annoyance, to say the least, will surely be felt by the parties concerned. Besides, a mistake of this kind is likely to prejudice the mind of the customer, and another article (however well-made) might not, perhaps, be received with favour; therefore, be exact. I wish now to direct attention to the illustration which appears on the next page and to the following directions for measurement.

No. 1.—With a tape measure ascertain the circumference of the head.

---

[19] Fig. 35.

No. 2.—Measure from the centre of the forehead (where the hair *should* be) to the nape of the neck.

No. 3.—Ascertain the distance from ear to ear across the forehead (see the lower dotted line).

No. 4.—Measure from ear to ear over the top (or highest) part of the head.

No. 5.—Note how many inches it is from temple to temple, round the back of the head.

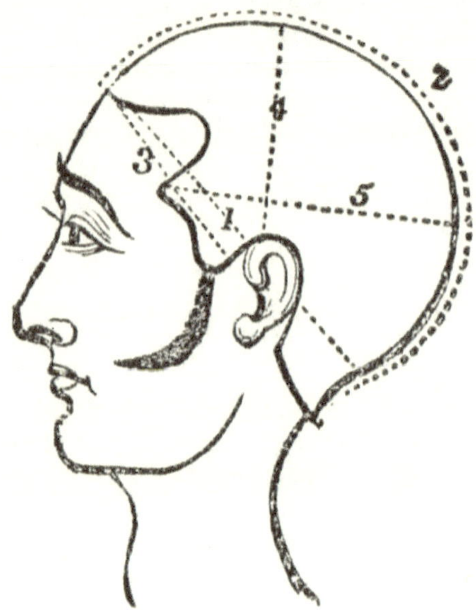

Fig. 33.

These directions are simple enough and only require careful attention; be very exact in writing down the figures, and observe the formation of the head. Of course, all these measurements are not wanted for a scalp (some scalps at all events), but the different kinds of work are so intimately associated that it is difficult to make any very marked distinction here upon the subject. Besides using a tape measure, it will be as well to cut out a paper pattern for a scalp. An expert might say there is no necessity for doing both, but I am not addressing myself to the advanced men in the trade, who do not stand in need of assistance from me. I direct my remarks more particularly to apprentices, improvers, and to beginners in general. To them I say—you cannot be too particular, therefore do not spare yourself a little extra trouble, as you may probably reap advantage from it before the job is finished. A paper pattern for a scalp comes in very useful at times, more especially when there are some intricacies to be noted. It need not be exactly a pattern, but still it should unmistakably show the outline of the patch which is to be covered. Having taken the dimensions, then, the next thing is to cut off a piece of hair for the colour. Your customer should be advised to wear his hair a convenient length for the purpose in view, (say) from two and a-half to three and a-half inches long. Fashion, of course, has much to do with the length of men's hair, but you cannot make a wig or scalp with hair so preposterously short as is worn by many at the present time—that is out of the question. The real hair as well as the "false" should be sufficiently long to allow of one combining with the other. There ought not to be any division, and the length of the hair must, as a consequence, be taken into consideration. Whether a crown is to be put in, or a crown and parting, should next engage attention; also, whether the parting is to be in the centre, on the right, or left side; if it is to be skin or transparent; and what kind of foundation. These preliminaries being arranged, I will proceed with the making of a scalp.

The scalp you are to make is without a patent parting, but with a crown either of silk or skin. If any parting is to be made on this scalp, it should not be clearly defined, but whether it be formed with weft or "knotted," the hair ought to be set closer than it is elsewhere. This, however, will be alluded to later on. Should a rather narrow scalp be all that is required, and the wearer's hair thick enough, a parting could well be made upon the head, some of the natural hair being trained to comb over and allowed to mingle with the hair of the scalp. Nothing could be better than an arrangement of this kind, where it is possible to adopt it. Attention must also be paid to the "set" of the hair upon the brow; if allowed to remain in slight disorder perhaps that would be the better way to wear it. At all events, a "wiggy" and cloudy aspect should be avoided.

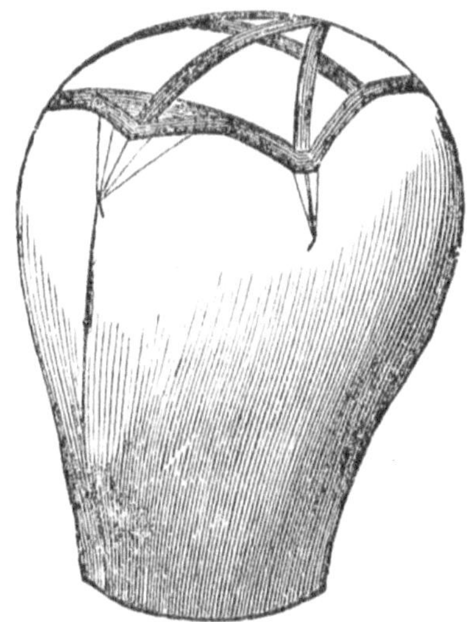

Fig. 34.

The mount represented above is, as I before stated, for a scalp with a crown, but without a patent parting. In reference to mounting, detailed instructions have frequently been given, which I need not here repeat. Take a clean, smooth, mounting block, and with a blacklead pencil carefully mark the size and form of the work taken in hand. Having done this, commence at the back by tacking on the galloon (which should be a little wider than that ordinarily used for fronts, bands, &c.), and with it follow the line marked until the ends meet. Arrange this so as to have half an inch or more to spare at both of the ends. Of course, in following the pencil marks with the galloon, you have found it necessary to use points so as to keep the shape, drawing the galloon at the same time moderately tight. You are now to hold the free ends between the thumb and finger of the left hand close down upon the block, while you stitch them through and through, so that when done they may be close and firm. Open the ends, gently hammer the sewn part, and take a few stitches to keep the ends in place. You are now to baste where it has just been sewn, observing to maintain an even roundness so as to fit nicely at the back of the head. Come now to the front and form the peak upon the forehead, but it should be more rounded and less pointed than is indicated in the engraving.[20] The sides are to be basted out as shown, and to impart a graceful curve, points are to be driven into the centre of the block and the galloon drawn inward as required. I will now assume that the outline of the scalp is formed; the galloon moderately tight and firmly held in place—and that it is ready for other matters to be proceeded with. Sew a piece of galloon from temple to temple; affix another piece at the sides (across the top) and then connect the front and back together. A glance at the illustration shows clearly what is to be done.[21] Springs are now to be attached, and for this purpose take a piece of watch-spring sufficiently long to reach from the forehead nearly to the crown, or quite to the edge of the crown if considered necessary. Two other springs are to be prepared extending from the side angles to join the centre one. At this point they are not to overlap, but must fit evenly and flat. Here, again, a reference to the engraving will indicate my meaning. It may be necessary to put two springs at the back also, especially if the scalp be rather large, otherwise, the patent crown might be found sufficient. The springs are to be somewhat flattened, so as to fit the mount exactly, for unless this be attended to, the scalp will not lie upon the head as it should do. They must now be filed or ground off at the ends, and tipped with kid, thin leather, or parchment, the whole neatly covered with galloon, and then sewn in their proper places. The next thing is to put on some silk net, carefully sewing it all round the inner margin of the scalp. Cut off, leaving an edge which must not extend beyond the outer line of the galloon. Fix this in place by means of the "herring-bone" stitch, and sew the net to all the other edges of the galloon and springs. I may observe that it is intended to cover this mount with weft, but were it to be "knotted," the edges of the net should be left rather long, then turned in, and firmly sewn to the outer line as previously instructed.

"Pen-knife" springs should now be attached.

They are, as before stated, made to open, and upon being closed, a small portion of the natural hair is shut in with what might be termed the blade. Here is the representation of a "penknife" spring (open), and it is drawn the exact size.

The scalp now in course of manufacture would require three or four of these fastenings, namely, one on each side towards the front, and one or two at the back in convenient situations.

Observe that these springs are intended to lie as flat as possible, being made with a slight concavity, which should go next the head. They must, consequently,

[20] Fig. 34.
[21] Fig. 34.

be arranged as "rights" and "lefts." Take a piece of galloon the width of the spring (that which is used for the mount will probably answer the purpose), turn in the ends, and sew over and over right round, *except* where the blade shuts in. In order that you may properly secure the covering, notice three small holes in the spring, through which stitches should be made. These details having been attended to, the springs are to be attached to the mount, and, I need scarcely say, they ought to be secure.

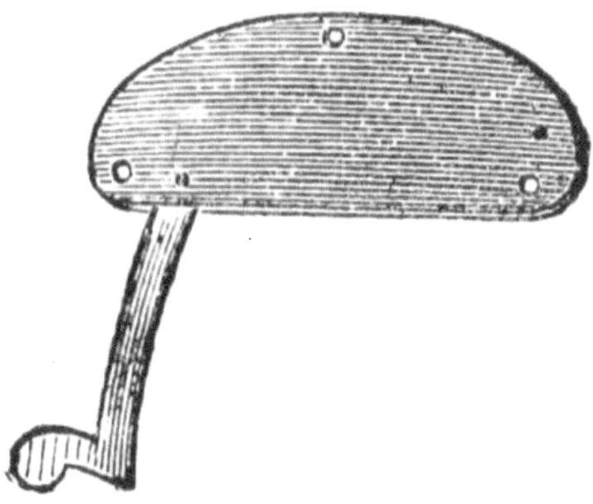

Fig. 35.

The hair is now to be put on, and the weft I presume is ready. Correct judgment, together with the requirements of the work, should, to a certain extent at least, guide you. As the rows of weft are arranged, so the hair will "set," and this should always be borne in mind. A properly made and well-dressed gentleman's wig is a "study," from which much is to be learnt, and young men in the trade should never allow such ingenious productions to pass unnoticed. Of the "cutting and dressing a gentleman's wig" I shall speak presently, and merely allude to it here for the purpose of showing the importance which attaches to a proper arrangement of hair in the first instance, whether it be woven or "knotted." Remember, as a rule, that in gentlemen's wig-making the hair should always be dressed to the face, but this effect cannot be produced without careful attention to the rows of weft, or "knots." However, in this instance suppose you adopt the following plan. Commence sewing on the weft at the back, at the lower edge of the galloon, and continue it all round; go round again, sewing the weft moderately close to the first row. It is important that these should be well and neatly put on. Continue sewing till you come to one of the angular places which is to be filled up, bearing in mind the preceding observations. Then pass on (without cutting the weft) to another and another, till all the corners are disposed of. If this be judiciously executed, you will then have a "clear field" to work upon, and may go on sewing the weft round and round until you approach the crown, when the rows must be a little closer together. While there is yet plenty of room, take the crown (silk or skin I am supposing it to be), sew the edges, as is done when putting in a patent parting, and fix neatly, yet firmly, in its proper position. Then go on with the weft, and finish off *upon* the crown, close to the hair.

Having done with the needle, the work is now to be pressed (and some of these observations apply to wig-making in general), about which you must needs be careful. The hair employed in this description of manufacture (short crop hair) is specially curled for the purpose, and in making gentlemen's wigs, hair of two, three, and sometimes four different lengths is used, so as to avoid cutting, if possible. It stands to reason that the hair put at the top of a wig or scalp should be longer than that in the neck, while at the sides the hair required is probably of a length something between the two. Therefore, when purchasing the hair, calculate the length before-hand, or, should it be in stock, cut it off at the roots before weaving or "knotting," if it is found necessary to do so. In pressing and dressing this scalp, I will assume that merely the points of the lower hair are to be removed, therefore push back with a comb the same as though you were about cutting a lady's hair, and remove the ends *with a sharp razor*. Even this must be done in a particular manner, and is to be produced by a kind of sliding motion. Let me tell you the object which is to be attained, that you may the more readily understand what and how to do it. The natural ends of hair are finer and more pointed than they would be if cut. They curl and combine more readily if left in their normal condition, with which ordinary cutting is likely to interfere: therefore the employment of a razor is to make the points resemble the original as near as possible.

Pressing, you can now perceive, is equally important, and should be done first. You must press the work, but not the hair—that is, the curl; for if you do that, the job will be spoilt before it leaves your hands, that's all! Therefore, press carefully; incline each section of the hair as it leaves your fingers to take up its proper position; do not injure the curl in the least, and endeavour to impart to it a natural and becoming appearance.

Another way of fixing the scalp is by means of a metallic spring (see Fig. 36), and it can easily be adapted to the purpose. The galloon which passes across the top could either be dispensed with, or arranged so that the spring, when covered, passes along unseen. The front of it could easily be made to come forward, while the corner springs (either front or back) must be reduced, or otherwise designed so as to keep the scalp well in shape.

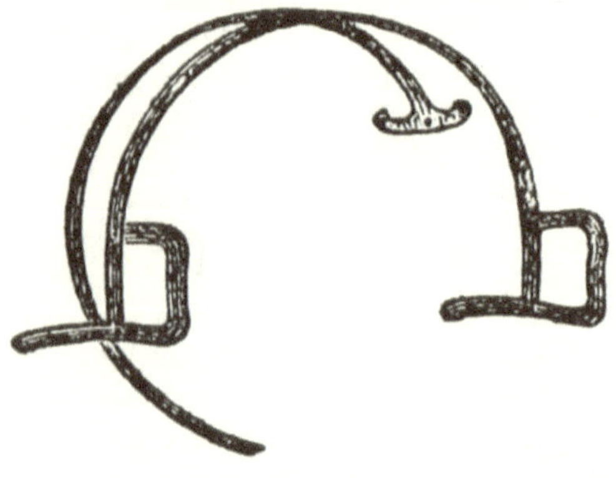

Fig. 36.

These springs, I may observe, are made to go across the top of the head, while others are constructed to go at the back, just below the bind of the hat. It is of the former description that I now speak. For making either a scalp or wig with a metallic spring it is best to keep some of these springs in stock, and when taking an order try them on, so as to get one that will be easy and comfortable. Heads vary in size, so do the springs; therefore, this mode of fitting a spring is essential. That part which extends from front to back is movable, and can be readily adjusted, while the behind part may be broken off at pleasure, the end, of course, being filed and covered in the usual way. With these preliminaries arranged, take a long piece of galloon, fasten on to a given point (say the front), and wrap round to the end, firm, smooth, and regular, holding the spring at the same time in the left hand; the upper edge of the galloon which is on the spring being covered with the lower edge of that which is free. Continue this from one end to the other and sew firmly. Now do the side-spring in the same way; cover neatly the centre at the top of the head, and sew wherever necessary. Of course, the spring will by this arrangement project at the sides, and extend down towards the ears. All this part, then, must be covered with weft, the hair well "set," pressed forward, and made to combine with the natural side hair of the wearer.

The mounting already shown is capable of numerous modifications, but the general directions remain the same. The form may be enlarged or diminished, it can be oval-shaped or round (or three-cornered if needs be), nevertheless, all the details must be carefully attended to if good workmanship be desired.

Baldness is not particular to age, neither does it assume any definite form; it varies upon different individuals. As a consequence the size and shape of scalps vary considerably, and the class of work is regulated not unfrequently by the purse. These deviations from any fixed rule, therefore, afford ample scope for the display of ingenuity and taste on the part of the boardsman; and to be a good wig-maker is a strong recommendation to first-class situations. Clever workmen, as I have stated before, do not stand in need of instruction, and were I to offer it some offence might reasonably be taken; but with apprentices and improvers, as well as those in business whose experience in the wig-maker's art is limited, the case is altered, and if I can be the means of helping them my task will not have been undertaken in vain.

To manufacture a scalp of a like description but with a silk or skin parting and crown inserted, proceed as follows:—Mark the outline of the mount upon a clean block and put on the galloon as before. Note the width and length of the parting, which should always be placed on the left side except when ordered otherwise, and arrange so that the centre of the crown will fall into its proper place. Having basted the galloon which marks the shape or outline of the scalp, you can then attach the piece which extends from front to back, and a cross piece right in front, if necessary (see illustration).[22] Notice the width of the parting, and in regard to this portion of the work, deal with the mount as instructed in mounting a front, paying great attention to the edge where it joins the forehead. About this you cannot be too particular. Now take the galloon and drive a point in the end of it, near

---

[22] Fig. 34.

to one of the basting-stitches, and conduct it upwards towards the crown; form the outline of the crown with it, and return to the fellow basting-stitch where it is to be cut off. I will now assume that you have the exact form of the parting and crown, the galloon being held in position by means of points driven into it at intervals. Sew the ends in their places, and baste the galloon, making a neat circle at the crown. Here the galloon will become puckered; the puckers are to be pinched together, sewn through and through, and made to lie as flat as possible. Having done all this, what, let me ask (in order that I may be clearly understood), is the object in view? It is to impart neatness to the work, and to conceal the margins of the parting and crown; it renders the scalp more durable, and when off the block the edges of the parting, &c., are neatly concealed.

The net and springs are to be put on, then the hair, and all finished off in a proper manner. Scalps of this description can be held in their places by means of a cement made and sold for the purpose (to which I shall presently allude), but I cannot help thinking that, after all, springs are preferable.

A better class of work is done upon gauze, and the best of all is made upon human hair foundations. Other materials for the purpose, of an inferior description, are used, to which I need not here refer, as the two kinds named are sufficient for my purpose. The gauze is very fine in texture, and can be mounted with galloon or not, just as it may be considered necessary. Of course, galloon affords additional strength to the article, and if lightness be not the chief requisition, I should say that gauze scalps were more durable when mounted. Here is an outline of one:—

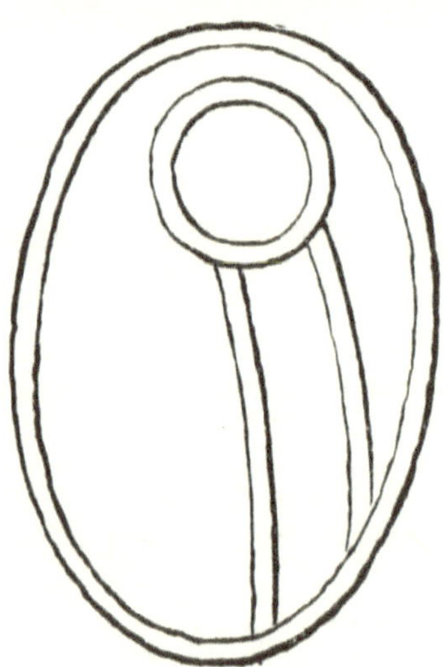

Fig. 37.

It will be seen that there is galloon all round, and to the parting and crown also. A mount of this character can be designed by omitting the latter altogether; it can be made with a crown only, or, with a parting in addition, as shown in the diagram,[23] but in that case, the piece of galloon which now marks a separation between the crown and parting should be omitted. This, of course, could easily be managed by putting on the galloon in the way just previously mentioned. A scalp of this kind can be mounted with white, drab, or other coloured galloon; it might be knotted either on gauze or net, with a human hair foundation parting and crown inserted. Indeed, the variations made in this description of manufacture are of a multifarious character, as may readily be perceived. The mode of attaching these scalps to the head of the wearer is by means of diachylon, or, what is better, the Pomade Toulouse, an adhesive substance easily softened by heat, or else "wafers," which are made sticky by a little moisture, and used as desired by the wearer.

Scalps with entire Human Hair Foundations cannot be excelled for lightness and a natural appearance. They are made of any size and pattern, with perfectly secured edges, so that no galloon or springs are necessary. They only require to be well and properly attached to the block by means of basting-stitches, and carefully—I might say artistically—knotted all over, the crown, or crown and parting, being done as the work progresses. Some exquisite pieces of workmanship are executed in this line by expert hands, their productions being well qualified to receive the name of "zephyr" which has been given to them by certain manufacturers. The mode of attachment is the same as that mentioned above, by means of cement or gum.

---

[23] Fig. 37.

CHAPTER XI.

Of Gentlemen's Wigs, and a few additional observations thereon—To
make a strong and durable Wig with woven Hair throughout—
Mounting a Wig—The Metallic Spring again—Various kinds of
Net used—Caution against using too much Hair—Sewing on the
Weft—The Crown made with Weft—The Parting formed with
Weft—Pressing the Work—Of Elastic Springs—The Wig complet-
ed.

It is now my intention to treat of Gentlemen's Wigs, and I think that, so far as general remarks are concerned, there is but little to add to my former observations on the subject. The approved method to be adopted for measuring the head, together with other necessary instructions, have been already given, to which the reader is referred. Like every thing else, gentlemen's wigs admit of considerable variation, and can be made to suit the pockets of all classes. Some customers are strictly economical; they do not so much care for appearances, their desire being to have a wig that shall be strong, durable, and low in price. Such men will wear a wig until it "goes foxy" (to use a trade phrase which fully explains my meaning). Some people, as they advance in years, have an aversion to putting on new things; preferring that to which they have become accustomed before a fresh, and, it may be, more elaborate article. This applies to clothing, boots and shoes, hats, &c., and why not to wigs? Therefore, in executing an order for a person who habitually wears one, notice every detail associated with that which he is wearing, and deviate as little as possible therefrom. Younger men, who lose their hair early in life, require to be much more particular; they wish to defy the scrutinizing glances of friends and acquaintances, and, as a consequence, seek to obtain that which is lighter, and of a more natural appearance. Price, it may be, is of the last consideration, for nothing, perhaps, would cause them greater uneasiness than to be told by some indiscreet associate, "Why, Jack, you've got a wig on." Men sometimes show their ignorance by making such foolish remarks; and I allude to it here to impress upon the reader how important it is to acquire taste, good judgment, and proficiency in business. I said just now that "gentlemen's wigs admit of considerable variation," and it is my intention to describe the manufacture of two kinds, namely, those which are intended to be worn for an indefinite period, and others that have to be renewed more frequently. That is to say, the buyer of a wig at thirty-five shillings would desire it to last for a longer time than he who purchases a more artistically made article at treble the price, and renews it every year.

I propose making a wig (in the first instance) of a strong and durable character, and with woven hair throughout. This description, either with or without patent crowns, or patent partings and crowns (of which more hereafter), I prefer making with weft, because I think them less likely to shrink than if they were knotted. Knotted work for lightness, weft for durability; at least, this is my opinion of the matter. It will be for the workman to decide which he considers preferable, and, as I shall give instructions how to proceed in either case, an opportunity will thus be afforded him to judge of the correctness of my assertion.

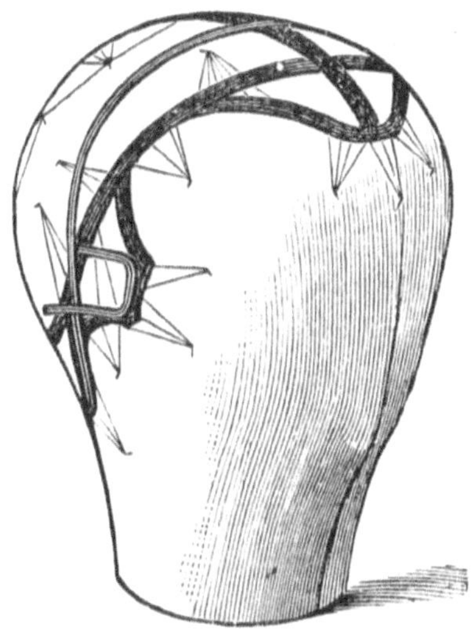

Fig. 38.

Take a clean mounting-block, and having your measurements properly written out according to previous instructions, pencil the outline of the mount thereon. Be very particular in marking details, because the galloon should follow every line. Having done this accurately, commence at the back of the block (in the neck) by driving a point or two through the galloon on the left side of the central line. Keep the galloon fairly tight with the left hand, following the pencilled markings, and hammer in points wherever it is necessary to do so. I will now assume that you have carefully made the proper curves at the ear and temple, and that you have reached the cut line on the block which is in the centre of the forehead. You have now to continue the galloon along the pencil markings on the opposite side of the block until the place from which you started is reached: drive in another point or two and cut off the galloon, leaving at least half an inch to spare upon the block. In foregoing instructions these "free ends" have also been alluded to; you are to pinch them well together, and, with a needle and silk, sew them through and through. The mount is now ready for "basting," but where you should begin is optional, and depends in a great measure on the style of mount. In this instance, I should begin in front; next the temples; then, round about the ears. The engravings which accompany these descriptions very clearly indicate details.[24] Having completed this part of the work, you will find that in various places the galloon

[24] Figs. 38 and 39.

is puckered; these you must pinch together, sew through and through, lay them down quite flat, and a stitch or two will hold them in their places.

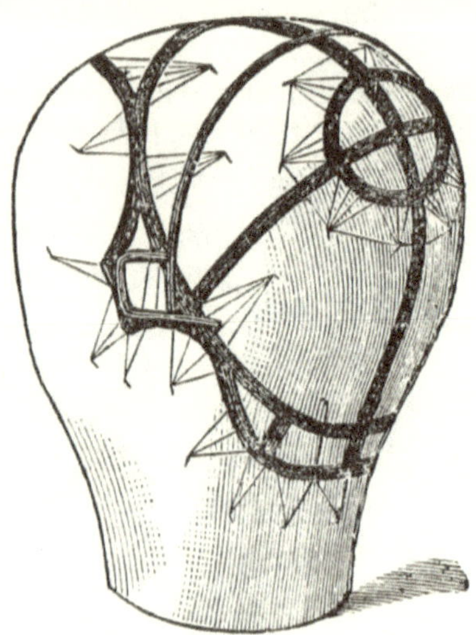

Fig. 39.

The first important step in making a wig is now accomplished. To be quite sure, go over your measurements again (I presume that you have done so before), and satisfy yourself of their exactness. Now, take the galloon and put a portion of it across the top from front to back; drive points through as before; cut off and sew neatly. A similar piece is to extend from ear to ear across the crown, which must be treated in a similar way. Having done this, take the galloon again, and, passing it under these cross-pieces, bring the ends to the front, pull it moderately tight, and sew down *upon* the galloon. This piece forms, as it were, a fillet round the head. Make a circle with the galloon, about two and a-half inches from the outer edges, to form the crown; in this instance I intend it to be made of weft, which will presently demand no little cleverness on the part of the wig-maker. This circle will have many puckers, and they are to be sewn down as before.

I have already alluded to metallic springs, and given an illustration of one.[25] The instructions then presented to the reader, must be borne in mind when an order is given for a wig, and also while the mount is progressing. Indeed, the spring ought to be placed in its appointed position when the mount is designed upon the block, and it should not reach (in any instance) to the lower edges of the galloon. The spring is to be covered as before, put on the block, and sewn in its place. With regard to other springs, which are used to keep the wig in shape, and thereby add to the comfort of the wearer, the engravings, together with previous instructions, will no doubt be found sufficient.

With the foregoing particulars, and the illustrations which accompany them, the learner can proceed to mount and make a wig. There is, in this class of work,

----

[25] Fig. 36.

much scope for ingenuity and thoughtfulness, and a well-made wig is not only creditable to the maker, but displays an amount of skilfulness which, to many, is surprising.

There are various descriptions of net used in wig-making to meet all requirements. For patterns and prices I cannot do better than refer the reader to either of Messrs. R. Hovenden & Sons' warehouses. To suit my own purposes, I find it sufficient to divide the net into two classes, viz., silk and cotton, of which, I need scarcely add, the latter is the cheapest; but for strength and durability, as well as neatness, the former is much to be preferred. The form and size of the mesh is not of any particular moment if woven hair has to be used; but when the hair is knotted the case is different, and, as the learner becomes proficient in his business, he will understand why some particularity in the choice of net should be exhibited by the worker, more especially when he takes delight in the excellence of his productions. I have said before that in manufacturing wigs, the "set" of the hair is all-important, and in knotting, the formation of the mesh is, doubtless, considered to have a great deal to do with it.

The mount being divided into sections by means of the galloon which passes from front to back, side to side, etc., enables the maker to sew on the net in parts, in preference to one entire whole. It is better to do this portion of the work in sections, not only because it is economical, but it is much more convenient. Commence (say) at the neck, by sewing the net to the innermost edge of the galloon, and you may arrange to cover one or both of the back divisions. Having sewn it along the edge securely, draw the net fairly tight, and stitch it to the nearest edge of the galloon which divides the front from the back. Cut off, but leave a sufficient margin to "herring-bone" afterwards. The front part of the wig may be covered in a similar manner. All edges of the galloon must be sewn to the net. I will now assume that the mount is covered except the points near the ears, the front peak, and, it may be, the nape of the neck. The angular, or odd pieces of net, will do exceedingly well for these. All being sewn to every available spot, the net tight and firm (not "baggy" —by all means guard against that), and free edges neatly "herring-boned" to the galloon, the mount is complete.

Of course, the hair selected for the top of the head, about the front and crown should be longer than it is at the sides and in the neck, therefore, two or three lengths of hair must be employed. A calculation ought to be made first, and the appearance, age of wearer, and so forth taken into consideration. As a rule, the makers of wigs put too much hair in their manufactures. The lighter they are, the better. Still, sufficient hair must be used to cover them, and much depends upon the fineness of the weft. Weaving some thirty yards of weft is, no doubt, considered a task by many, but unless it is fine throughout, more hair than necessary is likely to be consumed. An ordinary weaver should do at least a yard of wig-weft an hour, but professed weavers would do much more than that. The lengths of hair, then, having been decided upon, and their apportionment made, the weft should be completed without delay, before this monotonous part of the job becomes tedious. I said just now that too much hair is generally used, for I have known instances where three ounces or more of crop have been employed, in place of half, or two-thirds of that quantity, which would have suited the job much better. Here, then, is another cause of the "wiggy" appearance of which some people complain. Besides a general improvement in the article which adds considerably to the ease and comfort of the wearer, something is saved in the cost of material, which must not be lost sight of. True, the weight of hair depends in a great measure upon its length, but for ordinary purposes it should not be allowed to exceed two ounces, if possible.

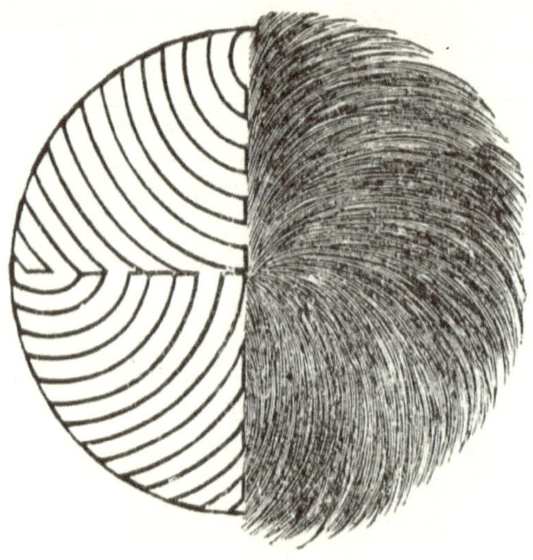

Fig. 40.

The weft being completed, begin sewing on behind the ears and in the neck; for this use the shortest hair. The first row, or, I might say, rows, of weft should, as a matter of course, be very carefully put on; indeed, *all* the margins or edges ought to receive the greatest attention, for if the hair be raised up and the work critically examined, a show of galloon would stamp it as bad at the very outset. Two, if not three rows of weft can be first sewn on before filling in the angles, and when that is attempted, both sides must be done uniformly. The angles (or points) behind the ears having been thus treated, the weft can be continued in lines until the neck part is all filled in. The sides should now be attended to, and, if the hair be sufficiently long, the front peak also. Commence sewing on the weft close to that which is already on the block, and this will be somewhere behind the ear. Stitch close to the edge of the galloon, and, as before, make two or three rows; then fill in the two sides. Bear in mind what I have previously said, which in this connection is worth repeating. It is this—remember, as a rule, that in gentlemen's wig-making, the hair should always be dressed to the face, but this effect cannot be produced without careful attention to the rows of weft, or "knots." Therefore, arrange the weft in such a way as to ensure this desirable result, and the pressing iron will do the rest. I now assume that all the angular places have been filled up, and that hair covers the wig up to the galloon which goes around the head like a band or fillet. You now require to use the second length of hair, and, probably it will do for both back and front; if so, go on sewing several rows of weft round and round at equal distances from each other. Not too close, otherwise the wig is likely to be heavy, and not very wide apart, or else the work will be flimsy and unsubstantial. Should you decide upon using longer hair for the top and sides than you do at the back, then the work must be done accordingly, by sewing half-way—backwards and forwards. The other half will have to be filled up in like manner; but, when the wig is taken off the block, the rows should appear as though they were sewn on in the way just before mentioned. I will now imagine that you are approaching the part marked out for the crown, and if you make any further difference in the lengths of hair to be employed, here you may begin with the longest, and continue up to the circle reserved for the crown. The hair used in this place may be of one length only, and can be sewn round and round until the lower margin of the crown galloon is covered with one or two rows of weft.

I previously stated that "I propose making a wig (in the first instance) of a strong and durable character, and with woven hair throughout;" but I have another object in view besides strength and durability. In all that I have written about "Board-work," I have addressed myself chiefly to apprentices and improvers, and in this particular instance I wished the young wig-maker to possess himself of a good specimen of his abilities. Indeed, I am now about setting a task which will try his ingenuity, and if successful in doing it well, he may justly feel proud of his work. It is to make a crown according to the illustration given on the preceding page.

A reference to Fig. 39 shows a wig mount, with the circular space left for the crown, which is, moreover, divided into four parts. In each of these divisions the weft (carefully and finely made for the purpose) is to be sewn according to the diagram Fig. 40. It will be seen from the covered half that each row of hair overlaps the other, and the greatest nicety should be exercised in working the exact centre, so as to conceal, if possible, every sign of weft. This is to be done by adroit workmanship, assisted by a warm iron and careful pressing.

To make a parting with the weft take a needleful of white cotton, mark the place for the parting, and the width it is intended to be. Simply make two straight lines from the crown to the temple, about an inch apart, and on the side the parting is worn. Having done this, remember that when sewing on the weft, it is to be turned back for an inch, and then returned again, so as to follow on in its proper course; these turnings and re-turnings being necessary (1) to bring the rows closer together, and (2) to make a division without showing the net foundation. Of course, a clear and distinct parting must not be attempted in this case, but just such a division as a hairdresser should be able to make on a gentleman's head with a brush only.

All being so far completed, the next thing to do is to *press the work, but not the hair*, otherwise the curl will disappear. Take a smooth, warm, pressing iron and begin, say, upon the left side, nearest the face. This will be at one of the angles, or points. Separate three or four rows of weft at a time, and of a convenient width, so as to hold the slip of hair firmly between the two fore-fingers of the left hand. Damp the weft *only*, with a small sponge, or the finger, at the same time inclining the curled ends to the face; press, lay the curl flat and leave it undisturbed. In like manner the whole of the work has to be treated, and when finishing off at the crown, see that its peculiar circular turn or inclination is well preserved. Having allowed a little time to elapse for all to get cold and "set," cut the basting stitches, and carefully take the wig off the block. Pull out all loose threads, examine your work, and see that everything is as it ought to be.

I have said that the block for this kind of work should exceed the circumference of the head by half an inch or more; this allowance is necessary, as it insures an easy fit, and provides to a certain extent for shrinking. Besides, should it prove to be a fault, it is one easily got over by means of an elastic spring, or springs. These springs are made of different lengths; but for a gentleman's wig, one would probably be two-and-a-half inches long, and it has to go at the back of the neck. Take the wig, turn the back part inside out, so as to get at the lower galloon easily. Cut a piece of galloon the same width, and full an inch longer than the spring. Mark the centre, and sew neatly (both edges) to the lower galloon, so as to form a casing for the spring. The stitching should not be continued to the ends. Now take a needle with doubled silk and fix it to one end of the spring; put the head of the needle foremost, and pass it through as though it were a bodkin. Draw the spring into position, and firmly sow first one end to the wig, and (having previously attached a second needle and silk to the other end) then the other. The degree of tightness required must be your guide, both as to the length of spring and amount of elasticity. Turn in the free ends of the galloon and sew neatly as before, until all is perfectly covered. Should a second spring be required, it is to be placed above, in exactly the same way, upon the fillet or band which goes around the head.

The wig is again to be put on the block, the hair cut *with a razor*, by a kind of gliding motion (to taper off the ends as much as possible), brushed and dressed. It is now ready for the wearer, and any other alterations in regard to trimming, etc., can be done upon the head, so as to adapt it to the features.

CHAPTER XII.

Of Gentlemen's Wigs (*continued*)—Difference between Woven and
Knotted Wigs considered—Instructions for Making a Knotted
Wig—Of the Parting and Crown—Of the Crown only—Pressing,
Dressing, etc.—A Superior kind of Wig Described, and Making
the same—The Transparent Parting and Crown—Sundry Import-
ant Details.

"Do you not think," said a gentleman to me one day, "that a wig made
with weft is rather old-fashioned?" The question can only be answered
in the affirmative, because knotted work has very generally superseded it, but,
I maintain, for a man to be clever in any trade or profession (and wig-making
forms no exception to the rule), he must be acquainted with all the rudimentary
parts. To be well grounded in the first principles of an art is, other qualifications
being equal, a sure precursor of success. Careful instructors are well aware of this,
and as a consequence, cause their pupils to undergo much preliminary training
before entrusting them with more difficult tasks. The medical and legal profes-
sions, painting, sculpture and music, chemistry, photography, and many others
might be enumerated to show the amount of technical instruction which must,
as it were, be drilled into a man before he is sufficiently clever to take a foremost
place in his profession. The art of hairdressing furnishes another instance of what
I am asserting, and the talented coiffeurs, who give expositions of their skill at the
different *concours* in Paris and London, afford examples of untiring energy, and
great attention to the most trifling details. The fact is, he who desires to be clever
must go plodding, plodding on, regarding nothing as too trivial for him to do, and
nothing (within reason) too difficult for him to attempt. Weft of one kind or the
other will always be in requisition; it is the key-stone of the hair-work trade, affords employment to the less skilful, imparts durability to false hair manufactures,
and is contributory to cheapness.

My inquiring friend could have put a similar question to me respecting the
metallic spring; but, let me ask, if a customer did not wish it, and it was not considered necessary by the wig-maker, why introduce it at all? The spring can be
left out, and other lesser springs substituted, as it is very much a matter of taste or
convenience. Some persons cannot bear the pressure of a metallic spring, which,
perhaps, is attributable more to the spring not fitting the head properly than to the
oversensitiveness of the wearer.[26] Yet I am under an impression that, for ordinary
wear, a wig with a well-fitting metallic spring across the top, or at the back of the

---

[26] See Fig. 36, and remarks thereon.

head (the latter especially) is both secure and comfortable; the wig retains its shape better, and, with weft, is much more durable. In matters of this description a great deal depends upon circumstances, and the arrangements made between buyer and seller. My desire is to give completeness to the work which I have undertaken; to have, as it were, a "word in season" for every emergency; to lead the pupil far on the road towards proficiency, and, having arrived there, he can well be left to look after himself, for he is no longer a learner, but a good boardsman.

To make a knotted wig, I will direct the reader's attention to Figs. 38 and 39, and request him to mount a wig in accordance with the instructions given therewith. He can mount it with, or without, the metallic spring, but in either case, care must be taken to affix springs of the requisite lengths, and in suitable places to keep the angles or points well in position. All the springs must be neatly covered, and put on *before* the net; in fact, as the wig is to be knotted, all galloon work should be done first, and the net affixed last. Silk net is to be used. In sewing, first stitch the net to the edge of the galloon in the usual way, and allow it to overlap the other edge before cutting off. Now that portion which overlaps is to be turned under and sewn, of course, to the second edge, and thus all the galloon becomes firmly covered with net. The same applies to the springs and with even greater force to the edges of the mount itself; and here it is necessary to be extremely careful, for when the job is completed and comes under the scrutinizing glance of the master, all wefts should be as regular and well-set as plants in a garden. There must not be inequalities, gaps, or other irregularities, all should be neat and trim. In this instance I do not propose inserting either a parting or crown. I rather prefer leaving the student to "try his 'prentice hand" in making them himself, at least, so far as he is able. My last wig was not intended for a clearly defined parting; neither is this one. The mount is now ready for the hair, instructions concerning which have already been given.

The course to be pursued when knotting the hair, is similar to that which was adopted with the weft—the object being the same. I would observe that, instead of turning in the net as before directed, the maker can (if he chooses) sew upon the galloon two or three rows of very fine wig-weft; one or two of them, however, must cover the edge of the net as well. Additional firmness being thus secured, the knotting can then be proceeded with. In knotting over or on the galloon and springs, coarser work, if considered desirable, may very well be done, but when it is executed on the net, the knots should be moderately fine and regular. The angles, or points of the wig, are to be well and properly filled in, and of course, all the hair should be drawn in the direction in which it is intended to lie. How close, or how far apart, the knots are to be placed is difficult to say. All net is not made alike; some meshes being large while others are small, and, of course, a fixed rule would not apply. Besides, all workmen are not painstaking or patient, therefore the knotter must observe closely the aspect of his work, and be the judge. Perhaps, with a moderately close mesh, it might be sufficient to knot hair in every other space; if this appears to make it too thick, reduce the number of hairs. This is a tolerably safe rule to follow, and a little practical experience will do the rest. The shorter hair is to be used for the neck and sides, the longer for the top; but in these matters such copious instructions are already given that the student cannot well make a mistake if he reads them attentively. He has merely to substitute "knots" for "weft," and the whole will apply to the job he has now undertaken.

As to the parting and crown, some of the details which have appeared are applicable here. As a clearly defined parting is not intended, it is merely necessary to implant, or knot the hair closer and finer on the side where the parting should be, than in any other portions of the wig. What division there is should be made with the brush (not with the comb), care being taken that the foundation is well covered with hair, and, of course, concealed from view. The crown is to be done last of all, and, if knotted upon the wig net, the design given for making a woven crown, Fig. 40, should be carried out as far as possible. The four sections are to be knotted in such a way that the hair of one falls over the other, while the knotting immediately in the centre should be finely and closely arranged.

Except it be for practice or an economical customer, I do not expect that such a crown will generally be made, because a silk, skin, net, gauze, or other crown can be obtained from the hair merchant, or patent parting maker, which, of course, imparts a better finish to the wig, and presents a more natural appearance. The illustration, Fig. 39, gives a circle adapted for either of the crowns just mentioned, and if a silk or skin one be employed no alteration in this part of the wig is required; but, should a transparent one be inserted, the cross-pieces of galloon must be omitted when mounting, or else cut away afterwards—the reason is obvious. If a transparent crown be inserted, it is optional whether a piece of thin skin (or other light material) be put on first, so as to prevent, to a certain extent, the effect of perspiration, but if a human hair foundation be employed, no such precaution is necessary. Whether a protecting substance be used or not, that part of the crown in which hair is implanted should be brought close to the inner edge of the galloon, and the free portion, *i.e.*, that upon which no hair appears, should lie flat on the galloon, to which it must be neatly sewn. Should any of the material on which the crown is worked overlap the galloon, of course it must be cut away. The vacant space (which will be just the width of the galloon) can then be filled in with weft, unless the net is properly arranged for knotting. But, should a non-transparent parting be employed, the galloon can remain as shown, and the whole be covered with the net used for the wig. In this case the edges of the crown are to be turned in very neatly before it is sewn in position, and, if possible, they ought to be concealed by means of the galloon, the intervening space is either to be filled in with weft, or else the hair can be knotted.

It will thus be seen that various methods of finishing off what might be termed the crowning point of a common wig can very well be adopted.

For Pressing, Dressing, Elastic Springs, &c., see remarks which have from time to time been made.

I have given such copious directions for making gentlemen's wigs, and dwelt at such length upon the various points essential to a good fit and the comfort of the wearer, that, perhaps, but little more need be said upon the subject. My instructions have been chiefly associated with productions that are strong and durable, for it may be accepted as a truth that when a man can execute the commoner work well, only a short time will elapse before he attempts, or is called upon, to do something better. Besides, as I have so frequently remarked, my instructions are more intended for learners than for skilled men. These do not stand in need of instruction; indeed, it would be impertinent to offer it to them; but with apprentices, improvers, and others whose opportunities for learning are few, the case is widely different. Though I have dwelt at some length on the manufacture of gentlemen's wigs—wigs that will endure a fair amount of every-day wear—yet a few particulars concerning the better-class article will certainly not be out of place, and might prove to be exceedingly useful.

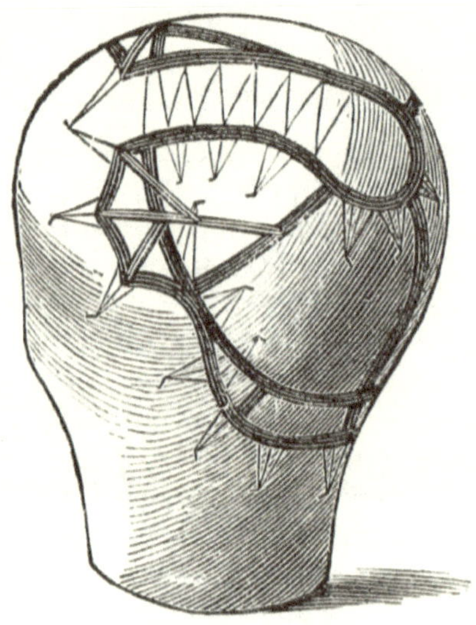

Fig. 41.

I must, therefore, again direct the reader to observe Figs. 38 and 39, and attentively read the instructions with which they are accompanied. Having done this, the above illustration is to be studiously regarded, and a marked difference will easily be perceived. The outline, as a matter of course, is to be preserved, and if the student feels so inclined, he can take a tracing and fill in the markings shown upon the others. There is no necessity for doing so, except that it impresses the mounting of a wig upon his memory in a more effectual manner. This wig is intended for a transparent parting and crown, the foundation of which may be either human hair, gauze, net, or such material as is generally used for the purpose. Before putting on the mount, it is best to provide the parting and crown, as well as the hair to be used for the other parts of the wig. Instructions as to length and quantity have already been given. My reason for saying that the parting and crown should be obtained *before* putting on the mount is, because exactness can be better observed. The edges of the parting work lie on the galloon to which it is sewn; the inner edges of the galloon must come close up to the margin of the implanted hair; "gaps" or vacancies should not be observable, but when the wig is removed from the block and examined, the parting and crown, being surrounded with the galloon, ought to look like a piece of artistic work well set in a frame. Of course, a silk or skin parting and crown may be employed instead of a transparent one, but then there is no occasion to leave the opening in front, as shown in the engraving.[27] In that case the galloon can pass round the head, be continued across, and the whole covered with net; this will impart strength to the wig—a transparent effect not being required.

To mount a wig for the transparent parting and crown, commence tacking on the galloon at the neck, the free portion lying towards the left hand. Proceed, keeping the galloon fairly tight till you reach the lower part of the ear; use more points, and continue till the top of the ear is approached; carefully curve the galloon and make a decided point in front of the ear. Then incline the galloon as shown on the temple, and up to where one corner of the parting is intended to be attached. Turn the galloon and trace the outline for parting and crown, returning to the angle near the centre of the forehead. Incline the galloon sufficiently low (but not lower than is absolutely required) and continue round the other side of the block till the starting-place is reached. Cut off, but see that there is at least half-an-inch of free galloon upon each side, which will presently have to be sewn together. You have now the outline galloon upon the block, which, after careful measurements, must be securely basted. (The "points" and basting stitches sufficiently well indicate this.) Afterwards, it will be found that the galloon is puckered in various places; pinch some of these together, sew through and through close to the block, and fix so as to obliterate all such indications. The inner galloon or "fillet" is next to be put on. This passes round the back of the head (at the neck) and is fastened upon the galloon at each side of the parting. A piece of galloon is then placed at the back, extending from the crown to the lower part of the neck; pieces of galloon being put at the sides, reaching from the top of the ears to the crown. Another piece of galloon is attached to the point upon the forehead, and joins the parting galloon in a straight line with the piece at the back. Springs are placed as shown in the engraving, or in such other positions as may be required. No metallic spring across the top can be used, and one at the back is best avoided, for with correct measurements, and perhaps one or two elastic springs in the neck, a close-fitting wig may well be assured. A reference to the illustrations will suggest other minor details, and, after all that has been said, the learner will know how to deal with them. The mount having been completed, the springs being neatly covered and placed in position, it now remains to put on the net. Given a transparent parting and crown, the other portions of the wig should be knotted. Indeed, all the better class of work ought to be so treated, though, in some instances, a little weft may be employed with advantage, especially if strength be required. However, in this instance, I have designed a knotted wig, the openness or closeness of the net being left to your own selection; regard always being paid to the kind of work you are going to do. When this part of the wig is completed the net ought to "fit like a glove," and wherever there is galloon, the net must be sewn to the edges of the same.

The knotting or insertion of the hair ought to be done with neatness and great regularity, and should be continued until nearly the whole of the wig is covered,

---

[27] Fig. 41.

with the exception of the parting and crown. Having dwelt at length on this part of the subject in other places, I cannot do better than ask the student to refer back for more complete details.

With regard to the transparent parting and crown, the reader is invited to look at Fig. 41, and he will perceive that the side galloons (on which the edges of the parting and crown are intended to be sewn) are securely held in position by some large stitches placed in a zigzag direction. These stitches can be increased or diminished at pleasure, or taken away altogether if such a step be desired, but I do not recommend it. They are intended to impart additional strength to the zephyr-like parting; to keep it from tearing, and to prevent its widening or stretching, as it most likely will do, unless something effectual be done to stop it. Most certainly there ought to be a "stitch" or "stay" within half an inch of the front of the parting, another should be placed where the parting ends and the crown begins, while a third might well be put mid-way between the two. There is a substance specially employed for making these stitches, called "Silkworm Gut," which can be obtained at Messrs. Hovenden & Sons' warehouses, and, as its name implies, is a kind of gut, white in appearance, and impervious to perspiration. The best white silk cord (about the thickness of coarse thread) is sometimes preferred; it can be renewed when thought desirable, and is, further, soft to the head. This arrangement, then, being completed, a piece of skin, used for the purpose, can be attached to the side galloons, but is not required when the foundation is made of human hair. The skin should not be allowed to reach the front of the parting, and must be turned upwards and inwards, so as to present a neat and even appearance at the edge when the wig is taken off the block. These preliminaries having been duly attended to, the parting and crown may now be put in position and sewn carefully, so as to avoid any wrinkles or puckering; it must lie flat, be perfectly smooth, and resemble the natural parting of hair as much as possible. Herein lies the art of the wig-maker—to imitate nature so skilfully that detection is almost impossible—a feat that is accomplished not unfrequently by some of the most skilful wig-makers of the day.

The larger portion of the mount being now covered with hair, and the parting and crown fixed, it remains for the intervening spaces to be filled in, which having been done the work is ready to be pressed. Instructions and remarks on this branch of the subject have already been given.

If possible, it is at all times desirable to try on a wig before giving it up to the wearer, and this remark has special reference to gentlemen's wigs. Elastic springs (in the neck) may or may not be put in before the fitting process takes place, and the finishing touches should, if required, be completed upon the head. The hair ought to be well combed and dressed to the face, and anything striking or likely to draw attention to the wearer (so far as the wig is concerned) must be studiously avoided.

CHAPTER XIII.

Of Ladies' Wigs, and important remarks thereon—Of Mounting and Making Ladies' Wigs—A well-balanced Wig essential—A Wig with Parting and Straight Hair throughout—All Weft to be concealed—Alterations—Of Wigs with transparent Partings—Mounting and Making the same—Shape of Head to be noted, together with any elevations or depressions—The Wig-block should be a correct Model of the Head.

It is now my intention to treat of ladies' wigs, but before doing so, I desire to make a few general remarks concerning them. If possible, I think it best to avoid making an entire wig for ladies' wear, if the customary plaited knot is intended to be worn behind, and my reason for expressing such an opinion will presently appear. Partial baldness among the female sex is not uncommon, but this defect can well be concealed by coverings specially made for the purpose. These pieces of ingenious workmanship, be they frontlets, scalpettes, fringes, partings, twists, chignons, curls, plaits, or what not, are easily and securely attached to the natural hair-growth, while a ribbon-bow, feather, flower, lace, cap, or other decoration lends a charm, and completes the coiffure. But when a wig is required, through the head being very considerably deprived of its natural covering, a difficulty immediately arises as to holding it securely in position, and this difficulty is increased by the smoothness of the scalp, caused, perhaps, through the nature of the ailment, or in consequence of the head being shaved. Besides, to promote the growth of hair, the shaving process should be frequently repeated, and, as a consequence, the smoothness remains until the hair has acquired sufficient strength and thickness to be permitted to grow. Then, as the hair increases in growth, the wig becomes more troublesome, and it is a welcome moment when the wearer can discontinue its use, and appear in a "short crop" which is, at the present time, so generally adopted for fashion's sake. But some cases of alopecia are known to have defied all attempts to restore the hair, while others, again, only lose it for a time, from no assignable reason. Instances like this necessarily require coverings for the head, which, in the case of gentlemen, are comparatively easy to deal with, but in long-haired wigs for ladies it is a different matter altogether.

Copious instructions have been given respecting board work in general, and the various manufactures therewith connected; and the ingenious tradesman will find but little difficulty, I am inclined to think, in devising a wig for ladies' wear, whether it be curled all over as a "friz," with or without parting, or frizzed in front only, with the hair short and partially straight behind. In either case the wearer would be at liberty to exercise discretion in the use of additional *postiches*, which may be employed with advantage, either as regards appearance, comfort, and what is perhaps no less important—additional security. In making wigs let it be a golden rule (1) that they *bind* well to the head, and (2) that the front and back parts be equally-well balanced, or, as nearly so as possible. I said just now that I thought "it best to avoid making an entire wig for ladies' wear, especially if the customary plaited knot is intended to be worn behind," and here is my reason for saying so: *It too frequently happens that wigs of this description are over-weighted at the back.* Consequently they slide away from the face, leaving the forehead bare. This, of course, is a fearful source of anxiety and annoyance to the wearer, and complaint is forthwith made to the tradesman who executed the order. The article is then returned perhaps as a misfit, or else to undergo certain alterations. These are carried out by additional depth being given to the front; necessitating, perhaps, the insertion of a new parting; the hair at the back probably will be reduced in quantity (and it may be shortened), the result proving, doubtless, satisfactory. *Why? Because the wig is now more evenly balanced, and consequently sits upon the head a great deal better.* Here, then, is the secret of making a wig feel comfortable—let it be well proportioned, and use no more hair than is necessary. I cannot conceive anything so distressing to a wearer as the feeling of anxiety and discomfort which a wig causes through evincing a strong tendency to slip down behind. This should be overcome, and a clever wig-maker can, if permitted to use his own judgment, prevent, under ordinary circumstances, such a *contretemps* taking place.

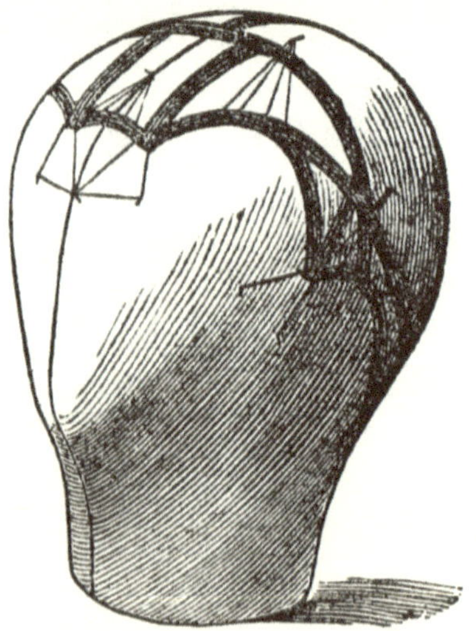

Fig. 42.

Respecting the mounting of a lady's wig, I wish, in the first place, to direct the learner's attention to what I have said upon the subject in preceding chapters, so as to avoid unnecessary repetitions. True the matter there refers to those worn by gentlemen, but the *modus operandi* is almost identical, and will apply, to a very great extent, in both instances. The clean block and pencilled outline, the putting on of the galloon, and attention to curves, the ears, temples, etc., must be equally well attended to—the principal difference being in the shape of the front part, to which it is requisite more particularly to allude.

In comparing Fig. 38 (mount for gentleman's wig) with the mount for a lady's wig,[28] the variation becomes apparent. A gentleman wears the parting at the side, but as a lady usually parts her hair in the centre, the front has necessarily to be somewhat differently designed. Let us suppose that a wig has to be made according to the design given on the preceding page, with a patent skin parting in front and long hair behind. The parting, I should say, ought to be five or six inches in length if straight hair is to be employed, and, perhaps, still longer should "a friz," or short curls be desired. Why? To preserve the balance as much as possible, of which I have already spoken. There might be (say, for example) two ounces of 14 and 16–inch hair in front, and two and a-half ounces of 18 and 20–inch at the back; and if the mount be made well forward there need not be any apprehension of the wig slipping off. But should the wearer wish to have a fringe on the forehead, with curls at the sides (either long or short), equality of weight must, nevertheless, be maintained, and the other portion treated accordingly. A well-balanced wig is, at all times, essential to success.

To make a wig, then, for straight hair only, mount it as previously instructed. Having fixed the galloon according to pencilled outlines, baste it carefully and put another piece of galloon across the top, which must extend from ear to ear. Next attach galloon to where the mount rises above the temples, pass it round the back like a fillet, and fasten on to the corresponding side. Prepare and cover the springs, and place in position as indicated. In the neck, just behind the ears, two other springs are to be attached, similar to those marked in Fig. 39. Galloon is also to pass from the top of the parting to the nape of the neck; a piece of broad ribbon on the top, between the two springs,[29] and the net being put on finishes the mount. Whether the hair shall be woven or knotted is optional, and in reference to both methods of affixing hair, instructions have been freely given in other places. If the former be decided upon it may be advisable to refer to page 72, *i.e.,* in so far as the front is concerned, but a somewhat different way must be adopted with the back. After filling up the neck and angular parts with the longest or most suitable length of hair, it will be found that there remains a more or less circular place at the back to be covered, and in order to do this properly the sewing should be commenced in the middle, and continued round and round (like making rings upon paper without removing the pencil), until the whole is filled in. The weft ought to be very fine and well spread, and in the *centre part* especially the rows need not be anything like close together. Indeed, rather than leave an unseemly opening, I have found it necessary at times to fill up the middle portion with short, fine hair, which, being concealed by the longer hair is no defect whatever. By such an arrangement, lightness is maintained, while the rows of weft are continuous and regular. The weft being measured, and a calculation made as to the space to be covered, the worker must then act accordingly. There are two principal points now to be mentioned. First, the cross-parting from ear to ear, which in the pres-

[28] Fig. 42.
[29] See Fig. 29.

ent instance I have designed should be formed with the weft. It requires some little ability to do this nicely, for the hair must be so placed as to conceal the weft, though still making a separation or parting. Some do it by adroitly covering with the hair all the weft except the last row, which, being closely woven and very fine withal, is sewn on the wig the wrong way, *but*, the hair being pressed into proper position, covers the weft, and effectually conceals it from view. There are other modes of attaining this object, but much depends on a man's ingenuity, for here is a difficulty which a clever workman must seek to overcome. Secondly, it is natural for some fine, short, more or less fluffy hair to grow in the neck; and here is the next trial of skill on the part of the wig-maker. No weft, of course, should be seen in such a noticeable place, therefore attention must be given at the outset to hide the lower row or rows, partly by skilful manipulation in sewing on, and also by means of the short hair to which I have just alluded. In effecting the concealment of the weft, attention should be given to the different kinds employed in the manufacture of *postiches*, etc.[30]

Referring to the illustration last given, I wish to observe that the mount there shown can be adapted to a transparent, instead of a skin parting, with very little trouble. An order might be taken for one of the latter description, and perhaps countermanded when the mount is completed in favour of one of a lighter manufacture. All that is necessary under such circumstances would be to cut away the lower-central piece of galloon; adapt the basting threads to the altered conditions, and connect with zigzag stitches.[31] Besides, alterations are not unfrequently required in wigs after they have been worn; and a wearer may wish for increased ventilation in it, through its causing the head to feel hot and uncomfortable; or other changes might be wanted which necessitate the insertion of a new parting. The requirements of people are various, but the ingenious workman seldom acknowledges a difficulty that (within reasonable limits) cannot be overcome.

To make a lady's wig with transparent partings, pencil the outlines upon a clean block, but, if possible, get the partings done before-hand; my reason for this I have already given. Exactness is essential, for, with the mount being made in one place and the partings (front and cross-partings) in another, a discrepancy *might* occur which is best avoided. I will suppose that the hair, partings, galloon, net, etc., are all ready to hand; the measurements carefully observed, and, perhaps, some other necessary details noted. Commence by tacking on the galloon at the neck, bring it towards the left ear, and then, over the temple to the side of the parting; turn, and continue the galloon as far back towards the crown as the front parting is intended to go. Turn again, and fasten off at the top of the ear, taking care to follow the line marked for the parting. A portion of one side of the mount is thus formed which can be traced by referring to Fig. 42. The right side should be done in the same way, and I need hardly observe that both sides must correspond exactly. Next place the galloon so as to extend from one temple to the other, and across the back of the neck after the manner of a fillet, but it must overlap (just behind the ear) that which was first put on. Another piece of galloon is next to be fixed in position across the top of the head, extending from one ear to the other.

[30] See Chapter V.
[31] Page 104.

With an obvious exception at the top, there will now be two galloons exactly the width and length of the cross parting, and two galloons in front also, exactly the width and length of the front parting. The professed wig-maker may raise an objection to the galloon remaining at the ends of the side partings; but in such places it will scarcely be seen, and by allowing it to remain much additional strength is given to the wig—no unimportant consideration with those of an economical turn of mind. But, as I have repeatedly stated, these lessons are not designedly for the very skilful, and it is a question whether the man who attempts to make a wig such as I am describing need refer to this at all. I imagine not, but there are learners, and to them instruction will always be acceptable. The springs (made of fine watch-spring) are to be neatly covered and placed in their respective positions. It is advisable to affix one on each side of the front parting, and the others where necessary to maintain the proper shape of the mount. The net should be put on next and sewn according to instructions frequently given before. Whether the hair is to be knotted or woven, the maker must decide, but perhaps the former is best adapted for a wig of this kind. Whether the partings should be attached before or after a greater portion of the hair is knotted or sewn on, is optional, so long as their proper adaptation is secured. Should they be of gauze or net, it may be thought desirable, first of all, to attach some thin skin, to counteract as much as possible the effects of perspiration and grease; but if the foundation be made of human hair, no such precaution is necessary.

I have before alluded to the different kinds of net used in wig-making, and there is also variety in galloons, some being white and some flesh-colour, as well as the ordinary brown. Bear in mind my remarks about ladies' wigs being well-balanced, and when measuring the head, carefully observe the shape. If smooth and round, two elastic springs in the neck will be absolutely necessary; but should the head incline to fulness (either back or front) these more or less prominent organs, speaking phrenologically, will perhaps give a "stay" to the wig, and the elastics may be considered unnecessary. A word or two concerning natural elevations and depressions may probably be useful. It has been previously stated that in mounting a wig the block must be at least half an inch larger round than the actual measurement; this is to allow for shrinking. Should there be any protuberances or "bumps" apparent, a similar elevation must be made upon the block, and, of course, exactly in the same position. This may be done with thin sheet lead, such as tea-chests are lined with; but should there be a depression, then the place upon the block must be filed or scraped away if necessary. The block is, as it were, the model; and with a good model to work upon, a perfect fit can almost be ensured.

I need not dilate upon any other styles of ladies' wigs, believing that I have said quite enough to enable a man to make almost anything that might be required.

CHAPTER XIV.

The Use of Leather Rollers in Curling Hair—Papering and Pinching
Hair with the same object in view—Plaiting Hair (for Coiffures)—
Of Razors, Razor Setting, and Razor Strops—Miscellaneous Rec-
ipes.

Besides the preparation of hair for making it into twists, curls, bandeaux,
scalps, wigs, etc., there are many other things to be done with care and
attention, and "Board-work" will not be complete without some allusion being
made to them. For instance, there is the curling of hair with leathern rollers. These
rollers are smooth, soft, round, and well adapted to the purpose. They make a nice
curl if properly manipulated, do not break the hair, and only the application of a
little warmth is necessary. For ringlet hair nothing can be better, no matter whether
it be real or false. Next to the employment of rollers, is the process of papering and
pinching the hair. A dexterous workman experiences no difficulty whatever in
rolling up a thin strip of hair (no matter whether it be long or short) with his thumb
and finger, and wrapping the usual three-cornered curl paper around it. But a
curling-peg is more generally employed. This is a round piece of hard wood about
six inches long, perfectly smooth, with one end much thinner than the other. The
reason is—should the hair be short, or a tight curl required, the small end must be
used, but if the hair be long, and a full, round, curl wanted, then the thicker portion has to be employed. The curl is made by rolling it round and round the "peg"
(beginning at the points and ending at the roots), and keeping it as flat as possible
all the time. Then hold the curled portion securely between the thumb and fingers
of the left hand, withdraw the "peg," and place the curl within the three-cornered
paper aforesaid, screwing up the ends to make all secure. When this is done, the
curl should feel perfectly round within the paper, the centre being equally as well
formed but hollow. Bear in mind what I have so frequently said before, that all
curls should turn to the face. Only a medium quantity of hair is to be taken for each
curl, and all ought to be about the same size. The curls are next to be "pinched,"
and, for this purpose, pinching irons are brought into requisition. If the hair be
somewhat new, and of good quality, the less heat that is applied the better, but
should it be otherwise much warmth and pressure is necessary. Old hairdressers
can recollect when the fronts and curls which came to be re-dressed had to be
baked (they were so numerous), and how trouble was caused sometimes, through
their being "overdone."

The papering should be done in regular order, and all quite cold before the
papers are removed. For dressing, a little oil (not pomade) should be used, and the

curls—if long or short ringlets—formed with the aid of a curl-stick or cold curling irons. True, they can be formed with the fingers, but the other method I consider best. Short, round curls, of course must be made with the fingers after a little frizzing, but these operations are difficult to explain in writing—they want practical illustration, which, now that we have societies and schools, is easily obtainable.

Concerning the beautiful art of plaiting hair for ladies' coiffures, the reader is informed that copious instructions are already given in my "Lessons in Hairdressing," and to that work he is respectfully referred.

Of razors and razor-sharpening much might be said, both as regards the instrument itself, as well as the proper mode of keeping it in order. Every hairdresser and barber knows when he is in possession of a good razor, and undoubtedly takes proper care of it. He is to be commended for this, as he simply follows the course adopted by those in other walks in life. Whether the old-fashioned description of razor is better or worse than the more modern "hollow-ground" I will not discuss, believing that a great deal depends upon the shaver, the nature of the beard, and the conditions under which the shaving operation is performed. Good practice in a barber's shop is the best school in the world for imparting a knowledge of easy shaving; while ordinary intelligence combined with shrewd observation, will go far towards making one a master of his art.

"It appears," observes a writer[32] on the subject, "that the choice of a razor may quite as well be left to the makers, as determined by the purchaser; however, it sometimes happens, that, exclusive of its goodness, the weight, the poise, &c., of a razor, are circumstances which seem to claim acquaintance with particular hands; and, with regard to these, every one will do well to suit himself.

"I have lately ventured, notwithstanding the long-established notion that weight is a very requisite property in a razor, to recommend those which were deficient in this respect; and I will embrace this opportunity to offer the reasons which influenced my judgment on the subject.

"It does not appear, upon considering by what means a razor acts, that its ponderosity can assist in the operation; the performance depending upon the condition of the edge, abstractedly from its weight; momentum can assist only where force is requisite; thus, in dividing a tough piece of wood, we find that the edge of a knife, however keen, cannot make its way; it becomes necessary, therefore, to use some instrument of more weight, which, being applied by an accelerated action of the arm, becomes equal to the task. The weight of all cutting instruments should be adapted according to the nature of their acting; and if the beard required to be hewn, or chopped off, doubtless, a hatchet, with a sharp edge, would answer the purpose better than a razor; on the contrary, if the beard can be erased by an unforced incision, which is certainly the case, an instrument of no considerable weight, with a proper edge, will always deserve the preference; for the hand, having nothing to overcome in point of weight, performs with more exactness and ease, than it possibly can, when feeling the oppression of weight in the instrument it has to manage."

---

[32] A Treatise on the Use and Management of a Razor, by Mr. Savigny.

As regards hollow-ground razors much can be said in their favour, and many in the trade consider them to be the best, but of this each man must judge for himself. I think that much depends on fancy, and what we are accustomed to, as well as to the mode of treatment. Sometimes it is requisite to put a long-used razor by for a time so as to restore its edge, and the following observations anent "Tired Razors" are *à propos* of the subject: — Barbers often assert that razors get "tired" of shaving, and that they will work satisfactorily if permitted to rest for a time. It has been found by microscopic examination that the "tired" razor, from long stropping by the same hand, and in the same direction, has the ultimate fibres of its surface or edge all arranged in one direction, like the edge of a piece of cut velvet; but after a month's rest the fibres rearrange themselves heterogeneously, crossing each other, and presenting a saw-like edge, each fibre supporting its fellow, and hence cutting the beard instead of being forced down flat without cutting.

Razor-setting cannot well be taught—it must, (like tuning a violin)—be acquired. Some persons are unable to set a razor with any degree of certainty, while others become recognised as clever in that branch of the business. The quality of the hone is an important consideration in razor-setting; it should neither be too hard nor too soft. The razor has to be rubbed from heel to point in the usual way, and *always turned on the back*. The edge should be tried from time to time upon the thumb or finger-nail, until it feels quite smooth and keen, it is then to be fixed or "set." This is effected by passing the razor to and fro, as lightly as possible and with single strokes upon the hone. Do this for a short time until the edge "bites" the nail as it were, when the setting is completed. Should it not do so, the assumption is that the setting has not gone far enough; the other extreme being when the edge is wiry, and then the setting is overdone. In either case the job is not satisfactory, as the razor is "not in tune," and will quickly require to be set again.

Stropping assists greatly in fixing the edge of a razor, and perhaps I cannot do better than quote what Mr. Savigny says upon the subject: —

"In strapping a razor, it is necessary to observe, that the thick or hind part bears upon the leather at the same time the edge does: for if the back is raised, the hand loses its only guide; in which case it could not fail of receiving some injury; but if the razor is applied flat, and the strap a proper one, ten or twelve strokes, on each side the blade, will be sufficient to give the edge its necessary refreshment.

"I have always given directions to draw the razor downwards, from the termination of the edge to the point; having experienced that this is the most steady manner the hand can act in; and it is an observation pretty well established, that any thing may be drawn to a much greater degree of exactness, than it can be shoved; and in the present case, were a razor to be pushed upwards along the strap, that is, from the point to the termination of the edge, there would be some danger of its turning on the rivet, and cutting both the leather and the fingers; to be as secure as possible in this respect, it will be well to place the hold just above the rivet, grasping at the same time the handle, and that part of the blade which issues from it.

"The manner in which a proper strap acts upon a razor must necessarily form an edge most suitable for the purpose, as it neither wears it so fast as the hone, nor confines its effects entirely to a flat; by the gentle manner in which it operates, and being in some measure yielding to pressure, it cannot leave that roughness upon the edge, which the hone, on account of its quickness, and the solidity of its surface, is commonly found to produce."

There cannot be two opinions regarding the importance of a good strop, and its being kept in proper condition, if the edge of a razor is to be considered.

For ordinary use, I give the preference to buff leather mounted upon wood in the old style, but there should always be a layer or two of common leather or other suitable substance between; otherwise there will be a hardness which, to say the least, is not agreeable. Softness and pliability should always be aimed at, and, doubtless, this is why many prefer a long piece of buff securely fastened to the wall. In preparing the leather for shop use, after having cleaned and thoroughly dried it, saturate it with olive oil, and then let it be well dressed with suitable razor paste. (If the leather is intended to be affixed to wood, it must be glued on first and time allowed for the glue to harden.)

Canvas strops are generally recommended for hollow-ground razors, but they are specially prepared in Germany, with the aid of suitable machinery. When unprepared, the canvas is exceedingly hard, and to adapt it for use, it should be filled with soft soap, the ends secured, and boiled for some length of time in a sufficient quantity of water. It is then to be pressed flat, scraped, and well rubbed with a smooth, round instrument until it becomes soft and pliable.

MISCELLANEOUS RECIPES.

Razor Pastes.

(1.) From jeweller's rouge, plumbago, and suet, equal parts, melted together and stirred until cold.

(2.) From prepared putty powder (levigated oxide of tin), 3 parts; lard, 2 parts; crocus martis, 1 part; triturate together.

(3.) Prepared putty powder, 1 oz.; powdered oxalic acid, ¼ oz.; powdered gum, 20 grains; make a stiff paste with water, q.s., and evenly and thinly spread it over the strop, the other side of which should be covered with any of the common greasy mixtures. With very little friction this paste gives a fine edge to the razor, and its action is still further increased by slightly moistening it, or even breathing on it. Immediately after its use, the razor should receive a few turns on the other side of the strop.

(4.) *Mechi's.*—Emery, reduced to an impalpable powder, 4 parts; deer suet, 1 part; well mixed together.

(5.) *Pradier's.*—From powdered Turkey stone, 4 ozs.; jeweller's rouge and prepared putty powder, of each, 1 oz.; hard suet, 2 ozs.

Obs.—The above (generally made up into square cakes) are rubbed over the razor strop, and the surface being smoothed off with the flat part of a knife, or a phial bottle, the strop is set aside for a few hours to harden before being used.

Shaving Pastes.

(1.) Naples soap (genuine), 4 ozs.; powdered Castile soap, 2 ozs.; honey, 1 oz.; essence of ambergris, and oils of cassia and nutmegs, of each 5 or 6 drops.

(2.) White wax, spermaceti, and almond oil, of each ¼ oz.; melt, and, while warm, beat in two squares of (white) Windsor soap, previously reduced to a paste with a little rose water.

(3.) White, soft soap, 4 ozs.; spermaceti and salad oil, of each ½ oz.; melt them together, and stir until cold. It may be scented at will. When properly prepared, these pastes produce a good lather with either hot or cold water, which does not dry on the face. The proper method of using them is to smear a minute quantity over the beard, and then to apply the wetted shaving-brush, and not to pour water on them, as is the common practice.

ESSENCE OF SOAP, SHAVING ESSENCE, OR SHAVING FLUID.

White hard soap[33] (in shavings), ¼ lb.; rectified spirit, 1 pint; water, ¼ pint; perfume (at will), q.s. Put them into a strong bottle of glass or tin, cork it close, set it in warm water for a short time, and occasionally agitate it briskly until solution be complete. After repose, pour off the clear portion from the dregs (if any) into clean bottles for use, and at once closely cork them. If the solution be not sufficiently transparent, a little rectified spirit should be added to it before decantation. A little spirit (fully proof) may be added if it be desired to render it thinner. If much essential oil be used to perfume it, the transparency of the product will be lessened.

Chiefly used for shaving, by travellers and others, to avoid the trouble of carrying or keeping a soap-box. By simply rubbing two or three drops on the skin, and applying the shaving brush, previously slightly dipped in water, a good lather is produced. The choice of perfume is a mere matter of taste, as with toilet soaps, 15 to 20 drops of essence of musk or ambergris, 1 fluid drachm of any of the ordinary fragrant essences or esprits, or 12 or 15 drops of essential oils (simple or mixed), per pint, are sufficient for the purpose, a corresponding name being given to the preparation; as "Essence," or "Esprit de Savon à la Rose," "Essence Royale pour la Barbe," &c.—*Cooley*.

ROSEMARY HAIR WASH.

Cold (boiled) water, ½ gallon; spirit of rosemary, 10 ozs.; eau de Cologne, 10 ozs.; glycerine, 2 ozs.; salts of tartar, 1 oz.; liquor ammonia, ½ oz. Colour with burnt sugar.

AMERICAN SHAMPOO LIQUID.

Take of sesquicarbonate of ammonia, and carbonate of potash, of each, 2 drachms; soft water, 1 pint; dissolve, and add the solution to a mixture of tincture of cantharides, 1½ fluid ounces; rectified spirit, ¼ pint; and good rum, 1½ pints; and agitate the whole well together, adding a little scent or not, at will. A commoner kind, in which the "rectified spirit" and one-third of the "rum" is replaced by water, forms the "shampoo liquid" often used by hairdressers, after cutting the hair.

A WASH FOR MOIST, LAX HAIR.

Take of essential oil of almonds, 1 fluid drachm; oil of cassia, and essence of musk, of each, ½ fluid drachm; rectified spirit, 2½ ounces; mix, and add gradually, with brisk agitation, 16 ounces of distilled water, in which 1 ounce of finest gum arabic has been dissolved. The hair and scalp should be slightly moistened with the liquid, and the hair at once arranged, without wiping, whilst still moist.

---

[33] Olive-oil (white Castile) soap, or almond oil soap is here intended. It should be moderately dry when weighed, next reduced to thin shavings, and then further desiccated by exposure to warm, dry air, but no artificial heat should be employed. By replacing a portion (say one-third) of the above with an equal weight of dry, white tallow soap (*i.e.*, curd soap) the "lathering" quality of the essence will be increased.

Washes for Dry, Stubborn Hair.

The best and most effective of these consists of glycerine dissolved in any fragrant distilled water, as that of roses, or orange or elder flowers, in the proportion of 1 to 1½ ounces of the former, to 1 pint of the latter. Some of them also contain 15 to 20 grains of salt of tartar per pint.

Egg Julep.

Egg julep, or saponaceous wash, is made as follows:—Rectified spirit, 1 pint; rose-water, 1 gallon; extract of rondeletia, ½ pint, transparent soap, ½ oz.; hay saffron, ½ drachm; shave up the soap very fine; boil it and the saffron in a quart of the rose-water; when dissolved add the remainder of the water, then the spirit, finally the rondeletia, which is used by way of perfume. After standing for two or three days it is fit for bottling. By transmitted light it is transparent; but by reflected light the liquid has a pearly and singularly wavy appearance when shaken.—*Piesse.*

Bay Rhum.

Tincture of bay leaves, 5 ozs.; otto of bay, 1 drachm; bicarbonate of ammonia, 1 oz.; biborate of soda (borax), 1 oz.; rose water, 1 quart. Mix and filter. *Piesse* says: "This is a very good hair-wash. It was first introduced in New York by those go-ahead scissors that 'abbreviate' the 'crown of glory.'"

Another.

Bay leaf otto, ½ oz.; magnesium carbonate, ½ oz.; Jamaica rum, 2 pints; alcohol, 3 pints; water, 3 pints. Triturate the ottos with the magnesium carbonate, gradually adding the other ingredients, previously mixed, and filter.—*Snively.*

To Allay Irritation of the Skin after Shaving.

Powder, either plain or scented, is the best counter-irritant after shaving, but as some persons give the preference to bay rhum, the following formula may be adopted:—Bay rhum (of the ordinary strength), 8 ozs.; rose water, 8 ozs.; glycerine, 2 ozs. Mix, and let it stand for a few days, then filter. Should this be found too powerful for general use, add more rose water.

Brilliantine.

A solution of castor oil in eau de Cologne, 1 part in 4. Another: Glycerine and eau de Cologne, of each 1 part; honey, 2 parts; rectified spirit, 4 parts. Another formula is as follows:—Castor oil, 1 oz.; esprit de rose, 1 oz.; spirits of wine, 2 ozs. A few drops of tincture of saffron to colour.

Marrow Oil.

Prepared (benzoated) lard, 3 lbs.; clarified beef suet, 1½ lbs.; palm oil, ½ lb.; yellow wax, 4 ozs.; castor oil, 1 lb.; olive oil, 1½ lbs.; ess. oils of bergamot, lemon, and cloves, of each, ½ oz.

Hair Oil.

Finest olive oil, 3 lbs.; castor oil, ½ lb.; ess. lemon 1½ ozs. To colour, steep 1 oz. of alkanet root (bruised, and tied in muslin) to every 20 ozs. Apply heat by means of a water bath, and filter.

THE END.

Lector House believes that a society develops through a two-fold approach of continuous learning and adaptation, which is derived from the study of classic literary works spread across the historic timeline of literature records. Therefore, we aim at reviving, repairing and redeveloping all those inaccessible or damaged but historically as well as culturally important literature across subjects so that the future generations may have an opportunity to study and learn from past works to embark upon a journey of creating a better future.

This book is a result of an effort made by Lector House towards making a contribution to the preservation and repair of original ancient works which might hold historical significance to the approach of continuous learning across subjects.

HAPPY READING & LEARNING!

LECTOR HOUSE LLP
E-MAIL: lectorpublishing@gmail.com

9 789354 205491